DON'T YOUR
HEART OUT

First UK edition published 1989

Originally published by Workman Publishing Company,
Inc., 1 West 39th Street, New York, New York 10018 in
1982, fully revised in 1987.

© Joseph C. Piscatella, 1982, 1987

British Library Cataloguing in Publication Data

Piscatella, Joseph C
Don't eat your heart out: a step-by-step guide to healthy
eating for a healthy heart.
1. Food. Low cholesterol dishes. Recipes.
     I. Title   II. Piscatella, Bernie
                641.5'63

ISBN 0-7225-1717-3

Published by Thorsons Publishers Limited,
Wellingborough, Northamptonshire, NN8 2RQ, England

Printed in Great Britain by Biddles Limited,
Guildford, Surrey

1 3 5 7 9 10 8 6 4 2

CONTENTS

COOKBOOK

INTRODUCTION

At the age of 32 I underwent coronary bypass surgery. It forced me to come to grips with the fact that heart disease is an epidemic. It doesn't just happen to "the other guy." It also forced me to recognize that certain aspects of my lifestyle, particularly my diet, were greatly responsible for my problem.

After the surgery, I set off with high hopes to eat in a healthier manner but soon became frustrated trying to figure out what was okay to eat. The standard "heart-healthy" diets were tasteless and unrealistic. In addition, none of them explained how to achieve permanent dietary change. They just said "don't eat that!" about every food I liked. No one could stay on these diets for very long. I found myself facing a very difficult problem: how to eat healthfully and still be a part of a modern lifestyle.

Don't Eat your Heart Out is a "how to" guide complete with recipes, menus and meal plans, that explains the practical application of low-fat, low-salt, low-sugar and low-cholesterol principles to contemporary diet. It tells how to combine healthy cooking with tasty eating. It is a blueprint for a permanently changing diet pattern.

Don't Eat your Heart Out has become the standard for a heart-healthy diet in over 4500 hospitals and is used in both cardiac rehabilitation and prevention programs. Its sensible, practical approach has made it a favorite of medical professionals and patients alike.

This revised edition contains current information on diet, including new research on the effect of olive oil and fish oil on cholesterol. While much of the information is new, the premise of the book has not changed: eating well and eating healthfully can be the same thing.

Joseph C. Piscatella

7

ACKNOWLEDGEMENTS

No one person produces a book such as this by himself. *Don't Eat Your Heart Out* would not exist were it not for the support and help of many people. In particular, I am grateful to Dr. John Nagle, Dr. James Early, Dr. Gail Strait, Dr. Denton Cooley, Dr. J. Ward Kennedy, Dr. Jack Copeland, Diane Gallagher (R.N.), Carole Gentry (R.N.), and Jean Macy (R.D.), all of whom gave generously of their time and expertise, providing valuable appraisals of the manuscript. In addition, Bonnie Nelson, Joan Imhof, Mary Piscatella, Em Stern and Pam Andrew furnished helpful editorial comment and suggestions for change. For their able and efficient secretarial support, my thanks to Flor Covey and Denise Johnson. A special note of thanks to John Vlahovich and Jim Gibson for balancing incredible patience with strong guidance in developing the graphic design of the book. And finally, my overwhelming thanks to my wife, Bernie, my most vocal critic and best friend, for her original contributions and for her untiring dedication to making this book become a reality.

CHAPTER ONE

THE HEART AND THE CORONARY ARTERIES

Until the time of my coronary surgery, I had felt no need to understand the function and the operation of the heart. Its health, much like freedom, was taken for granted. With the shock of surgery, however, came the desire to understand more about the heart. Suddenly, I was hungry for information about its functions, about the role of the coronary arteries, and about the complex arrangement of blood vessels in the circulatory system. I knew that the heart had to first be understood before an appreciation of the role of coronary heart disease could be gained.

THE HEART

The word "heart" is one of the most frequently used words in the English language. It is a word with many meanings which has been used throughout the ages in history, music and literature to describe love and affection, "to win her heart"; courage or spirit, "lion-hearted"; the core or vital part, "the heart of the matter"; a capacity for sympathy, "a heart of gold"; and as an expression of affection, "dear heart." These, along with ace of hearts, heart crops, the game of hearts, heartache. . . are all secondary meanings of the word.

9

One would think that with the number and the richness of the secondary meanings, the prime definition of "the heart" would be spectacular. Alas, it is not. The dictionary definition is simply "a hollow muscular organ which by rhythmic contractions and relaxations keeps the blood in circulation." This is certainly an adequate, if vastly understated, definition, but it does not truly capture the nature of this wonderful organ.

The heart is what the heart does: it is a pump. Pure and simple, pumping is what the heart is all about. Certainly there are many physiological complexities concerning the heart, such as cellular structure, electronic impulses, oxygen sensitivity and so forth. But when these complexities are removed, the essential nature of the heart remains. . . it is a pump. To describe the heart merely as "a pump," however, is akin to describing Mt. Everest merely as "a mountain" or the Amazon simply as "a river."

The heart is not just "a pump" — it is THE PUMP! Every day this unbelievable organ pumps 2100 gallons of blood continuously at the rate of over one gallon a minute through some 60,000 miles of blood vessels to reach over 300 trillion body cells. In order to accomplish this monumental task, the heart must beat over 100,000 times a day. At this rate, in an average lifetime the heart will pump over 135 million gallons of blood in more than 2½ billion heartbeats, and that is just when it is resting. It can pump six times its resting volume during exercise!

This pumping is such an amazing feat that its magnitude is often difficult to comprehend. Two and one-half billion heartbeats. . . It's like talking about government budgets. The figures are too large to be realistic. Perhaps that is why the heart is taken for granted by most people and often is not appreciated until a problem occurs.

Many misconceptions abound about the heart. Upon learning of the awesome amount of work that is required of it, I assumed that the heart would be rather large. It is, in fact, quite small, about the size of a clenched fist, and usually weighs between seven and twelve ounces, depending upon the size of the person. By comparison, the heart of a bull elephant can weigh over 50 pounds.

A second misconception concerns the location of the heart. Most people believe, as I did, that the heart is located in the left breast. But in actuality the heart is located in the center of the chest directly behind the protective breastbone. Before my coronary surgery, I gave no thought to the location of the heart; but now, smug in my newly acquired anatomical knowledge, I smile inwardly each time I stand in Seattle's Kingdome and see 60,000 people sing the national anthem with a hand over their left lung.

A third misconception generally held concerns the shape of the heart. The heart is simply not "heart-shaped." It does not remotely resemble the classic valentine heart. While it may come as a shock to romantics and candy manufacturers alike, the heart is really shaped like. . . an eggplant! Suspended in its protective sac, the pericardium, the heart looks exactly like a grocery store eggplant in a plastic bag. Can you imagine Valentine's Day with chocolate eggplants and eggplant-shaped boxes of candy? For some people, myself included, this might take "truth in advertising" one step too far.

HOW THE HEART WORKS

The human body is made up of over 300 trillion individual cells. Each of these cells is a life unto itself, and each has a metabolic need for oxygen and nutrients in order to produce energy and new cellular material. Each cell also has a need to expel waste products and carbon dioxide. In this respect, the life of each cell parallels the life of the body as a whole.

The process of "in with the good, out with the bad" must occur continuously if the cells are to remain healthy. Any disruption in the process — too little oxygen and nutrients going in or too little waste and carbon dioxide coming out — will negatively impact their good health. Of critical importance to each cell is an uninterrupted supply of oxygen, for no cell can live more than 30 minutes without oxygen. Some cells, notably those in the brain and in the heart, live for a considerably shorter time when deprived of oxygen.

For this reason blood is constantly being circulated throughout the thousands of miles of arteries, arterioles, capillaries, veins and venules which make up the blood vessel system. The blood vessels are the vehicle by which oxygen and nutrients are delivered to the cells and by which waste and carbon dioxide are removed from them. It is much like an enormous freeway system which is connected to a city. On the incoming roads are found a flow of food trucks going into the city; on the outgoing roads are found garbage trucks hauling refuse from the city. The life of the city depends upon the constant movement of the trucks on the freeway. Any slowing or stopping of this traffic could result in famine or disease. It is the same for the body. Blood must circulate constantly throughout the blood vessel system. But it can only do so as a result of the pumping action of the heart.

While the heart is considered a single organ, biologically it is two separate pumps which work together: the right heart and the left heart. The two pumps are completely separated from each other by a wall of muscle. Each heart has two chambers, the atrium, or holding chamber; and the ventricle, or pumping chamber. The right heart receives the blood containing waste products and carbon dioxide in the right atrium. This blood, called "poor blood" is low in oxygen. (Contrary to social myths concerning the blue-blooded rich, "poor blood" is characteristically blue; "rich blood," blood high in oxygen, is characteristically red).

After the right atrium is filled, the poor blood is sent to the right ventricle, which in turn pumps it to the lungs. This is a fairly easy activity for the heart due to the low pressure maintained in the lungs. Only an easy pumping action is required, and that fact is reflected by the relatively thin walls of the right ventricle.

Once the poor blood is in the lungs, it is cleansed of carbon dioxide, takes on oxygen and is transformed into rich blood. The rich blood then moves from the lungs into the left heart, where it is received and stored in the left atrium and is subsequently passed to the left ventricle. The left ventricle is the powerhouse pump of the heart. It is the chamber which will pump the blood to distant parts of the body, under high pressure and against much resistance, through arteries and capillaries which may be only 1/2500 of an inch wide.

Resistance to blood flow is a product of the diameter of the blood vessel. The smaller the blood vessel, the higher the resistance. This pumping takes tremendous power. As such, the left ventricle is a heavily muscular chamber with thick walls measuring one-half inch in width. The pressure necessary to drive the blood out of the left ventricle is so great that if the aorta were opened in the neck, a column of blood would spurt out to a height of five or six feet. Intense pressure is essential in order to keep the blood circulating.

Even from this simplistic description of the purpose and the function of the heart, it is easy to understand the importance of cardiac health. When the heart is healthy, it can pump needed oxygen and nutrients to the farthermost cells and can promote good health for the body. When the heart is not healthy, its pumping ability is diminished, and ill health can result. The heart — this small, misshapen, and wonderfully powerful organ — is essential to life. Its health cannot be taken for granted.

THE CORONARY ARTERIES

While the heart is often viewed as the key element in the delivery system — the pump which keeps the oxygenated blood circulating — its own dependence on oxygen and nutrients is often overlooked. The heart is a super-organ in terms of its capacity for work and its efficiency. However, like all other organs and body tissue, it also needs a constant supply of oxygen and nutrients; it cannot operate without fuel. The cardiac muscle has a need to be served, and that need is met by blood which flows through the coronary arteries.

I had assumed that the heart was somehow nourished by the thousands of gallons of blood which pass through its chambers. This is not the case. In spite of the large volume of blood which the heart processes, it must, like the rest of the body, be served by arteries. Only the blood which reaches the heart through the coronary arteries can provide nourishment.

The two main coronary arteries which originate from the aorta are the right and the left coronary arteries. They lie on the surface of the heart and divide into smaller branches so that every portion of the heart has a blood supply. The right coronary artery nourishes the right side of the heart and has branches which extend to the back of the heart. The left coronary artery has two main branches: the left anterior descending branch which nourishes the front of the heart, and the left circumflex branch which carries blood to the back of the heart. These arteries surround the heart and actually curl around its surface like a crown. It is this crown-like characteristic that gives the arteries their name. In Latin crown is "corona."

In establishing the coronary arteries as the supply line for the heart, nature has developed an efficient delivery system. Each time the heart pumps rich blood through the aorta to the body, a portion of that blood is syphoned from the aorta through the coronary arteries back to the heart itself. It's like a commission that the heart pays itself for the work performed. Of the rich blood that is pumped into the aorta, 95% is supplied to the body and 5% finds its way back to the heart. Every time the heart pumps, it works to nourish itself. The fact that only 5% of the rich blood is sufficient to meet the needs of the heart is due to the ability of the heart to extract more oxygen per milliliter of blood than any other organ of the body.

Although the location of the coronary arteries and the 5% commission system are designed in

THE CORONARY ARTERIES

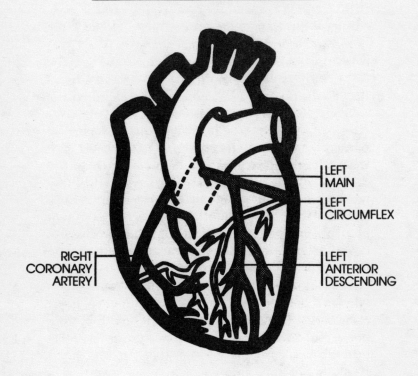

combination to provide all areas of the heart with an adequate blood supply, that design is fraught with potential problems. The arteries themselves are extremely small, about the size of cooked spaghetti. Thus, any blockage or obstruction can easily reduce the blood supply to the heart.

In addition, unlike other arteries in the body which are protected by muscle tissue, the coronary arteries are located on the surface of the heart. They are afforded no protection by the heart itself.

The coronary arteries are forced to move, stretch and kink as the heart muscle contracts and relaxes. This constant movement can cause much wear and tear, expecially at the points where the arteries bend, and can make them susceptible to small tears on the inside wall of the artery. These tears often become important in the development of artery blockages. The fact that the arteries are not protected and can easily tear is a major reason why a blockage can develop. And the fact that coronary arteries are very small is a major reason why such a blockage can impede the blood flow and cause a heart attack. These arteries, the weak link in the circulatory chain, are the real Achilles' heel of man.

CHAPTER TWO

CORONARY HEART DISEASE

Coronary heart disease is found in epidemic proportions today.

Basically, coronary heart disease is a condition in which the blood flow to the heart is restricted due to the buildup of blockages on the inner walls of the coronary arteries. This condition is the product of a disease called atherosclerosis, which is derived from the Greek *athere*, meaning "mush," and *skeros*, meaning "hard." Literally translated as "hard mush," it is an apt description of the fact that an arterial blockage begins as a soft, mushy accumulation of fat and cholesterol and ends as a deposit of hard, encrusted material.

Atherosclerosis progresses silently, often without any outward manifestation of its debilitating effects. As it does so, blockages begin to form and the arterial walls begin to thicken. The channel through which the blood flows becomes more and more narrow. In addition, the arteries themselves lose their ability to expand. The resulting impediment to blood flow can seriously impair cardiac performance. Should the blood flow be completely stopped, a heart attack will take place.

WHO GETS CORONARY HEART DISEASE?

Coronary heart disease is mostly identified with middle-aged and elderly people. While this is the age when the disease is made manifest, many young people also carry arterial blockages. In some infants the disease is detectable at birth, and studies have illustrated that coronary artery blockages may even be present in a fetus. Dr. Forest H. Adams of the Pediatric Atherosclerosis Clinic at UCLA has demonstrated that traces of the disease are common in American children by the time the tenth birthday is reached. Dr. Charles J. Guleck of the University of Cincinnati has found that elevated cholesterol levels — a prime indicator of the disease — can be found in children as young as eight years old. In addition, research involving autopsies performed on children killed in auto accidents have confirmed that coronary artery blockages exist even in young children.

Significant studies were also conducted during the Korean and Vietnam wars involving young adults. These confirmed that youth offers no immunity to coronary heart disease. The young men studied, whose average age was 22, were in excellent health until the time of their battlefield death. Their autopsies revealed that despite their young age, many cases of severe coronary heart disease existed. It was concluded that some 35% of these young men were well on their way to heart attack.

It is often thought that females are generally immune to coronary heart disease, but statistics illustrate that sex provides no ultimate immunity either. Males between the ages of 30 and 49 are 6.5 times as likely to develop the disease as females of the same age. This is probably due to the female

20

production of estrogen, a sex hormone which seems to protect against coronary blockages. As the female ages, however, her risk of developing coronary heart disease increases rapidly. Shortly after menopause her odds become equal to those of the male.

No one is immune to coronary heart disease. The insidious aspect is its silent progression, its ability to remain undetected until it has reached an advanced stage. It is only when the blockage seriously restricts the blood flow to the heart that the disease becomes noticeable. Often it is too late. While a heart attack may be described as "sudden," the blockages which produce the attack do not "suddenly" grow, but develop silently over a period of years. Although blood cholesterol measurement may indicate the probability of the disease in a person, there exists no practical, fool-proof early detection device.

Like most people, I had relied on an annual physical examination to disclose any potential heart problems. This exam always included a resting electrocardiogram. Unfortunately, a resting EKG will generally not disclose a blockage in a coronary artery until that blockage obstructs some 90% or more of the channel opening. Since an EKG is taken at "rest" when the heart is not under a heavy workload demand, the results may be "normal" whether the channel is 100% clear or 20% clear, as long as the heart is getting enough oxygen to sustain its resting beating pattern. It is only when the artery is obstructed more than 90% and the blood flow is impeded to the point where the heart has difficulty in sustaining a normal resting beating pattern that the EKG will show an abnormality. Four months prior to my coronary surgery I had received a resting EKG as a part of my annual physical. It showed no abnormalities.

Either my 95% blockage had totally developed within a 4-month period, which would have been highly unlikely, or it had developed over a period of time but had not as yet been large enough to show up on my resting EKG exam. Obviously, the latter is what occured. So, while my physical examination indicated that all was well, in reality atherosclerosis was in an advanced stage in my coronary arteries. This same situation has occured with other people as well. Not too long ago a prominent mayor of Chicago died of a heart attack as he was leaving his cardiologist's office after an examination in which his resting EKG was normal!

THE DEVELOPMENT OF
CORONARY HEART DISEASE

The coronary arteries are the only channel through which oxygenated blood is supplied to the heart. The exact sequence of events leading to the formation of blockages in those arteries is unknown. However, it is known that at birth the artery channel is smooth and that blood flows through it unimpeded, much as water will flow through a new pipe.

The coronary artery is lined with a smooth tissue, the intima, which by its nature helps the blood to move freely. Soon after birth, minute cracks begin to develop in the intima, the result of the constant movement of the coronary arteries as they twist and flex each time the heart contracts and relaxes. And with the heart beating some 100,000 times in a single day, it is not surprising that the wear and tear on the coronary arteries would produce such a result. When a crack does occur, blood cells and clotting material are rushed to the wound in order to repair it. As happens with external cuts or scrapes, a "patch" of new cells covers the wound and soon a protective scar is formed. Coronary artery cracks are common, and consequently each of us carries many coronary artery scars. Few of these scars pose a significant health hazard for the heart.

But a hazard does arise when the blood contains a high level of fat and cholesterol. The bloodstream then not only deposits blood cells and clotting material for repair purposes, but fat and cholesterol as well. The latter are quickly absorbed by the cells which surround the crack. As more and more fat and cholesterol are deposited and absorbed, the surrounding cells are forced to multiply rapidly in order to maintain the absorption rate. The result can be a wild, cancer-like growth of new cells which soon become swollen to the bursting point. The accumulation of these new cholesterol-filled cells is called a fatty streak, a protuberance which thickens the artery wall much as accumulated rust and corrosion can thicken the inside of an old water pipe.

The cells which constitute the fatty streak sometimes become stable and cease growing. In such a case they may not cause significant disruption of blood flow to the heart. But should the cells continue to absorb fat and cholesterol, the fatty streak can grow from the artery wall like a cancerous tumor and can constitute a dangerous impediment to the blood flow. This impediment is called a blockage or a plaque. It is estimated that well over 50% of all adult males in the United States today harbor one or more of such coronary artery blockages.

The natural consequence of coronary disease is a heart attack. In the situation where a blockage is large, or where a series of blockages exist, the blood supply to the heart can be curtailed to the point where the heart can no longer function normally and a heart attack results. Often even moderate sized blockages can be responsible for a heart attack.

If the blockage itself develops a crack in its hard exterior which allows the blood cells to come in direct contact with the fat and cholesterol, a clotting action will take place and frequently an enormous blood clot will be formed. The blood clot can act as an extension of the blockage, and the combination of clot and blockage may be of such size as to completely obstruct the artery channel and stop all blood to the heart. When this happens, a heart attack can result. In some instances the blood clot will break free to float in the blood stream. Should this floating clot become lodged with another artery blockage to stop blood flow, a heart attack can again be the result.

THE RESULTS OF
CORONARY HEART DISEASE

Coronary heart disease commonly causes four cardiac conditions. The first is angina, or angina pectoris, which in Latin means a "pain in the chest," and is the result of the heart muscle receiving insufficient oxygen to maintain its workload.

For many people, angina is a sharp pain in the chest, jaw, neck, arm or shoulder. For others, it is a discomforting sensation of tightening in the chest or heavy pressure behind the breastbone. It was described to me by one cardiac patient as "like having an elephant sit on my chest." Frequently angina is misinterpreted as a gas pain or an indigestion that will not go away. In my case, it was a burning sensation in the area of my lungs.

24

Whatever its manifestation, the pain of angina is generally sufficient to force a person to curtail his physical activity. For many people angina dictates a lifestyle moderation which precludes physical activities. In jogging, tennis, or for some people just walking up a hill, the heart is called upon to pump blood at an increased rate to those muscles which require oxygen. A jogger's legs, for example, may demand six times the amount of blood when running as when at rest. This increased demand in workload usually poses no problem for the heart. But when coronary artery blockages prevent the heart from receiving sufficient oxygen to maintain its high workload, angina becomes the warning sign to the body that the heart is in trouble.

Usually a person experiencing angina will be required by the pain to stop the activity, and the heart is allowed to return to its slower beating pattern. With the workload reduced, the oxygen requirement is dimished and the angina generally disappears. Sometimes drugs are needed to produce relief from the pain. Angina is a principal indication that coronary artery blockages exist and are of sufficient size to warrant concern about a heart attack.

The most common result of coronary artery blockages is the heart attack, also referred to as a myocardial infarction or MI. A heart attack takes place when the blood supply to the heart is completely stopped and an area of the heart muscle is without oxygen for too long a period of time. When this happens, the area affected suffocates and dies. The dead area can be large or small; however, once it dies, it remains dead. There is no healing or rejuvenating process which will restore the original muscle. Scar tissue replaces muscle tissue. Unfortunately, scar tissue does not have the ability to contract, and it is useless in the pumping activity of the heart. The scarred area consequently causes the heart to lose some of its effectiveness as a pump.

Congestive heart failure can occur when a heart attack has reduced the pumping power of the heart so that blood in the veins leading to the heart becomes backed up. A heart attack often causes significant scar tissue to form in the area of the left ventricle, the principle pumping chamber. When this happens the left ventricle may no longer have the ability to pump vigorously. But if the right ventricle is without scar tissue, it will continue to pump blood into the lungs at a rapid rate. The difference in pumping abilities of the two chambers may cause blood to back up in the lungs and in the veins, disrupting the normal circulatory flow and causing distension of the tissues and a leaking of fluid into the abdomen and the extremities. The swelling due to abnormally large amounts of fluid in the body tissue is called pulmonary edema. The liver and the kidneys are susceptible to damage when edema takes place, and a painful death can occur.

After an area of the heart muscle dies and scarring takes place, the muscle area which borders the scar is often in a half-alive state. It is injured, yet alive and receiving a supply of blood, but that supply is so inconsistent that the muscle area is always on the verge of death. It very much resembles a drowning man who is gasping for breath. Often in this situation the muscle will panic.

Instead of following the master electric rhythm sent out by the heart to establish the heartbeat rate, the affected muscle area begins to generate its own electrical rhythms in an attempt to increase the heartbeat rate and to gain more blood flow for itself. The new rhythms may be strong enough to override the master rhythm, which is usually about 72 beats per minute, and the heart can race wildly to 150 or 250 beats per minute. This condition is called tachycardia. Where the heart enters completely into undisciplined, uncoordinated contractions in excess of 250 beats per minute, the condition is called fibrillation. In either case, the heart muscle can be seriously damaged and death can result.

FOCUSING ON THE REAL PROBLEM

The consequences of coronary heart disease are serious and often fatal. Much effort and money have gone into the medical research involving angina, heart attack, congestive heart failure and fibrillation. Much media attention has been given to the tragic impact of these coronary problems on the lives of millions of people. And many physicians have spent countless hours helping their cardiac patients to cope with coronary heart disease.

While the consequences of the disease rightly demand our attention, it is imperative not to lose sight of the real problem: atherosclerosis, the cause of coronary heart disease. If we are to have any control over coronary heart disease and its consequences, we must first exercise control over the development of atherosclerosis itself.

This can be achieved only if individuals take action to reduce their risk of atherosclerosis before the disease becomes evident. The beginnings of the disease are found in the small tears in the intima which are a product of the human condition. About that we can do nothing. But its festering development is the product of elevated fat and cholesterol levels in the bloodstream, a situation in part caused by our national diet pattern. About this we can do much.

Without preventive measures, the disease is allowed to develop slowly, almost imperceptibly, over a period of time. It is like the progressive pinching of the fuel line until, no more fuel being available, the auto engine suddenly dies. It is the same for the heart when its fuel line, the coronary arteries, become blocked. It too, suddenly dies.

CHAPTER THREE

DIET IS A CARDIAC RISK FACTOR

The German poet Goethe once wrote that "Man is what he eats." This statement made no sense to me until my coronary problem forced me into a better understanding of the relationship between diet pattern and cardiac disease. It was only then that Goethe's insight could be fully appreciated.

Many health professionals today consider the contemporary Western diet to be the single most important factor in the development of coronary heart disease. They view our national diet as influencing a number of other life-threatening diseases prevalent today, such as cancer, high blood pressure, diabetes and stroke.

The problem is that what we eat bears little resemblance to what we need to eat for good health. Dietary decisions are based upon impulse, convenience, economics, status, taste . . . on a number of influences other than nutritional value. The Western diet consists of too much fat and cholesterol, too much sugar and alcohol, too much salt and too many calories. One nutritionist categorized it to me as consisting basically of "sweet and salty fat." The ramifications of our national diet have not been good for coronary health. As Dr. John W. Farquhar, Director of the Stanford Heart Disease Prevention Program has stated, "The Western diet may be hazardous to your health."

The relationship between diet and cardiac health has long been recognized by the American Heart Association. Since 1961 that organization has been clamoring for a change in the way Americans eat. More recently a comprehensive study was concluded by the United States Senate's Select Committee on Nutrition and Human Needs which resulted in the establishment of national dietary goals. These goals are intended to, among other things, reduce the high incidence of coronary heart disease and heart attacks in Americans.

The Committee has called for a reduction in the amount of unhealthy elements consumed by Americans, notably fat, cholesterol, salt, sugar, alcohol and total calories, and for an increase in the consumption of fresh fruits, vegetables, and whole grains. The recommendations specifically include:

>A reduction in fat from 42% to 30% of total calories.

>A reduction in saturated fat from 16% to 10% of total calories.

>A reduction in cholesterol from 600 milligrams to 300 milligrams per day.

>A reduction in refined sugar from 18% to 10% of total calories.

>A reduction in salt from 8,000 milligrams to 3,300 milligrams per day.

The Committee also recommended a diet with less red meat and whole milk; fewer processed foods; and fewer non-nutritive foods, such as candy, soft drinks and alcoholic beverages. Dr. Mark Hegsted, Director of the Human Nutrition Center of the Department of Agriculture, has stated:

"The diet of the American people has become increasingly rich — rich in meat, other sources of saturated

*fat and cholesterol and in sugar . . . The diet we eat
today was not planned or developed for any particular purpose. It is a happenstance related to our
farmers and the activities of our food industry. The
risks associated with eating this diet are demon-
strably large. The question to be asked, therefore
is not why we should change our diet, but why
not? . . ."*

These observations apply equally to Western diet
as a whole.

FAT AND CHOLESTEROL

A diet rich in saturated fat and cholesterol has
been identified as a major risk factor for coronary
heart disease. As Dr. Nagle succinctly sum-
marized the problem for me, "If you remember
nothing else about the relationship of diet pattern
to your cardiac health, remember these things:
>A diet pattern which is high in saturated fat will
 raise the cholesterol level of the blood.
>Where blood cholesterol levels are high, so is the
 risk of coronary heart disease and heart attack."

The Clinical Evidence

Much of the very early research concerning the
impact of dietary fat and cholesterol upon the
development of coronary heart disease was conducted on rabbits, dogs and cats. It illustrated that
a high-fat diet caused both elevated levels of blood
cholesterol and fatty artery deposits to occur in
these animals. Diet pattern was found to be the
principal factor in the elevation of blood cholesterol.

A certain amount of difficulty existed in as-
sessing the importance of the test results due to
the fact that the basic metabolism of the animals
used differed so greatly from that found in hu-

mans. Some researchers said the results were significant; others said that they had little meaning. It was subsequently decided to conduct these same tests using the Rhesus monkey, an animal with a basic metabolism quite similar to that of humans. In the test a monkey was fed a high-fat diet which was similar in fat and cholesterol content to the modern Western diet.

After being on this diet for 2½ years, the monkey suffered a massive heart attack and died. During the autopsy it was discovered that he had developed multiple coronary artery blockages. His heart closely resembled that of a human with severe atherosclerosis.

The notable point was that under normal circumstances the Rhesus monkey would not have been susceptible either to coronary heart disease or to heart attack, for neither are part of the natural animal condition. But this monkey did suffer a heart attack, one which the researchers concluded was induced by diet. The test findings clearly illustrated that the high-fat diet produced elevated cholesterol levels, which in turn contributed to the production of coronary artery blockages.

A number of studies and field tests involving humans have been conducted since World War II. One of the first studies was initiated in 1947 by Dr. Ancel Keys, a pioneer in cardiac research, at the University of Minnesota. In this test 281 businessmen in their 40's and 50's were studied over a 15-year period. During that time, some of the businessmen had heart attacks; some did not.

It was found that the men who had heart attacks had a significantly higher amount of cholesterol and fat in their blood than did those who did not suffer any heart attacks. Dr. Keys concluded that a direct relationship existed between a high level of cholesterol in the blood and a high incidence of heart attack. A person with a high blood cholesterol level, it seemed, was much more likely to have a heart attack than a person with a low blood cholesterol level. This was the first time that cholesterol was linked to coronary heart disease in humans; however, the study did not concern itself with diet pattern.

Other research projects followed. Among the most famous was the Framingham Study, started in 1948 by the Public Health Service. In this project, conducted over a 12-year period, some 5,000 adults were studied. The conclusion drawn was similar to that of Dr. Keys findings: the cholesterol level of the blood was the most significant factor in determining the risk of a heart attack.

Many other tests and studies were conducted which indicated again and again that a relationship existed between elevated blood cholesterol and heart attack. The results of a series of studies involving over 4,000 men concluded that a man with a cholesterol level of 260 had four times as much risk of a heart attack as a man with a cholesterol level of under 200. The consensus from these many tests was clear: the higher the cholesterol level, the greater the risk of heart attack.

It was not until the early 1950's that the role of diet as a risk factor was seriously examined. Again it was Dr. Keys who played an instrumental role. He developed a study of three groups of Japanese, each of whom were living in a different environment. Differences in heredity and physiology, which were evident in his prior studies, were set aside in this study, allowing Dr. Keys to concentrate on the differences in the diet patterns and in the cholesterol levels of the three groups.

The first group consisted of Japanese who lived in Japan. They ate a traditional low-fat Asian diet. This group had a low blood cholesterol level and a low incidence of heart attack. The second group were Japanese who lived in Hawaii. Their diet was a mixture of the low-fat Asian diet and the contemporary Western high-fat diet. The second group had higher levels of blood cholesterol and a higher incidence of heart attack. The third group were Japanese who lived in Los Angeles. They consumed the Western diet exclusively. Their blood cholesterol levels and their incidence of heart attack were much higher than the second group, and were significantly higher than the first group.

Dr. Keys concluded that the blood cholesterol level was influenced directly by diet pattern. This conclusion, coupled with his previous finding that elevated blood cholesterol is linked to an increased incidence of heart attack, opened the door to the modern medical approach to diet as a risk factor for coronary heart disease.

Another notable research test, the Seven Country study, was one in which diet, cholesterol levels, and frequency of heart attack were measured in communities in Finland, Greece, Italy, Japan, the Netherlands, the United States and Yugoslavia. In all, some 12,000 men in the age range of 40-49 years old were tested and observed. The study illustrated that cultures in which fat made up a significant percentage of total caloric intake were also cultures which demonstrated a high incidence of coronary heart disease. Thus, the Netherlands, where 40% of the diet was fat, had a far greater incidence of coronary heart disease than did Japan, where the diet was only 9% fat.

A further study done in Europe divided the continent into two distinct geographic areas based upon dietary patterns. High-fat Europe, with a diet similar to that of the United States, consisted

34

of the British Isles, Germany, Holland, Scandinavia, Belgium, Northern France and Northern Switzerland. This group was categorized as a "beer and butter" culture, and their diet pattern, while differing in national foods, was uniformly rich in fat. Low-fat Europe, on the other hand, exhibited a diet pattern which was lower in fats. This group, categorized as a "wine and oil" culture, consisted of Spain, Italy, Southern France, Southern Switzerland, and Greece. The study illustrated that a high level of blood cholesterol and a frequency of heart attack existed in high-fat Europe, while just the opposite existed in low-fat Europe. It concluded that blood cholesterol levels and incidence of coronary heart disease cut across geographic and ethnic boundaries where similarities in diet patterns did the same.

One additional study deserves comment. During the Korean and Vietnam Wars, autopsies were performed on American and Asian servicemen. All of these servicemen were young, about age 22, were fit and were without health problems. The American servicemen autopsied showed consistent evidence of coronary artery blockages already in evidence, while the Asian servicemen had relatively few blockages. The salient difference between these two groups was their respective patterns. The Americans ate a high-fat diet; the Asians, a low-fat diet. The evidence from this study corroborated the conclusions of the many other studies: diet pattern does have an impact, positively or negatively, on the development of coronary heart disease.

The Role of Cholesterol

Cholesterol has frequently been identified as the principal culprit in the development of coronary heart disease mainly because it is the chief component of artery blockages. The result is that cholesterol has received exclusively "bad press" and is perceived by the general public as a dangerous substance.

In truth, the role of cholesterol is not totally negative. Indeed, cholesterol is necessary to the normal chemical process of the body. Produced primarily in the liver cholesterol is utilized in cell wall construction. It also serves as an insulator between cells that are receiving electronic signals from the brain, thereby preventing an electrical short. No cell could survive without cholesterol.

The liver is not the only source of cholesterol. It also enters the body through foods that are eaten. This is dietary cholesterol, and it is found in foods of animal origin such as beef, pork, lamb, shrimp, organ meats and egg yolks. Many of these foods also contain saturated fat, a type of animal fat that causes the body to increase cholesterol production. Thus, a diet rich in animal foods (and therefore rich in dietary cholesterol and saturated fat) can cause blood cholesterol levels to rise. The more cholesterol in the blood, the greater the risk for coronary heart disease.

Cholesterol Levels

Blood cholesterol level is a key indicator of cardiac risk potential. The amount of cholesterol in the blood is determined by a blood test and is expressed as a number. This represents the number of milligrams (mg) of cholesterol in one deciliter (dl) of blood. For example, a person who has 275 milligrams of cholesterol in a deciliter of blood would have a cholesterol level of 275.

The higher the blood cholesterol level, the greater the potential risk for coronary heart disease and heart attack. According to the Farmingham Study, a person with a cholesterol level of 260 has four times the risk of heart attack as a person with a level of 200. The opposite is also true: the lower the cholesterol level, the lower the risk. Indeed, a study by the National Institutes of Health has shown that a 1% reduction in blood cholesterol level results in a 2% reduction in heart attack risk.

A relative scale has been established to define the relationship of cholesterol level to cardiac risk. Historically, a level of 300 and above constituted a high risk, while 200 and below represented a low risk. The normal or acceptable range used in the United States had been 225 to 275, with a mean of about 250. Today, however, many physicians no longer consider this to be a true indicator of risk potential because of the wide range involved. In addition, they've concluded that what Americans define as "normal" is considered excessively high in other parts of the world. In Third World nations where many people are vegetarians, the normal cholesterol range is 100 to 140. In the Mediterranean, Latin American and the Orient, normal is a range of 150 to 180. The normal mean level for Americans is 250. But in Italy it is 175, in Japan it is 163, in India it is 146, and in Peru it is just 137.

According to the National Institutes of Health, the cholesterol risk is more accurately like the following:

AGE	RECOMMENDED LEVEL	MODERATE RISK	HIGH RISK
2–19	Less than 170	170–185	Greater than 185
20–29	Less than 200	200–220	Greater than 220
30–39	Less than 220	220–240	Greater than 240
40 +	Less than 240	240–260	Greater than 260

Types of Cholesterol

In addition to the total amount of cholesterol in the blood, attention must be paid to the types of cholesterol that make up that total. There are two main types: one is harmful and considered "bad" cholesterol; the other is healthful and considered "good" cholesterol.

The chief distinction between good and bad cholesterol involves their chemical packaging. All cholesterol is insoluble in water, so it cannot be transported in a pure state via the bloodstream. It must first be combined with fat and protein molecules in order to become soluble. This combination, or chemical package, is called a lipoprotein.

One type is called a high-density lipoprotein, or HDL, and is described as a "good" cholesterol. An HDL which is primarily protein and contains very little fat, is very stable from a chemical viewpoint and will not come apart easily. Thus, should an HDL escape the bloodstream and penetrate an artery wall, the package will remain intact and the cholesterol will have very little chance to come in direct contact with the artery. In such an instance, the HDL will generally return to the bloodstream without causing damage. A high level of HDL's in the blood enhances cardiac health. The best way to improve HDL level is through a regular program of aerobic exercise.

A low-density lipoprotein, or LDL, on the other hand, is predominantly fat and contains very little protein. Unlike an HDL, an LDL is not a stable chemical package and comes apart quite easily. For this reason, it is described as "bad" cholesterol. Should an LDL penetrate an artery wall, the cholesterol could be released and become embedded. When this happens, the start of an arterial blockage could occur. LDL is what lines the artery wall and forms blockages. The higher the LDL level in the blood, the greater the risk for arterial buildup. Because of this, many physicians believe that its measurement is important in predicting the potential for future heart attacks. LDL's are very sensitive to diet and are increased by foods rich in saturated fat and cholesterol.

While it is an oversimplification to state that HDL is "good" cholesterol and LDL is "bad", this relationship is basically correct. HDL works to minimize the harmful effects of LDL by causing the body to excrete LDL. In fact, HDL helps to prevent the arterial buildups that LDL can cause. At birth, a person has equal amounts of HDL and LDL. But as a result of a diet that is rich in saturated fat and dietary cholesterol, most Western adults have four times as much LDL as HDL. And this is an important reason why coronary heart disease is of major consequence today.

The Role of Fat

The amount of dietary cholesterol a person consumes does have some bearing on his or her blood cholesterol level. While dietary cholesterol is important, dietary fat provides a more significant problem for most people.

Fat is one of the main classes of food essential to the body (the others are protein and carbohydrate) and has an important role to play in good health. Because it is a more efficient fuel than either protein or carbohydrate, it is a concentrated source of energy. The body stores fat as an energy reserve and draws upon it when extra fuel is needed. In addition, fat insulates the body against heat loss and cushions many organs against injury. Indeed, fat has a legitimately important role to play in the healthful functioning of the body.

The problem with fat in the Western diet involves the amount and type consumed. We eat a lot of fat because it is a basic component of our foods. We like it because it provides flavor and texture to what we eat. Because it is digested slowly, fat also helps to satisfy our appetites. Foods with high fat values include red meats such as beef, pork and lamb; processed meats such as luncheon meats, frankfurters and sausage; dairy products such as milk, butter and cheese; margarine; cooking oils; commercially baked goods such as pies, cookies and doughnuts; fast food fried in fat, such as hamburgers, chicken and French fries; and convenience foods such as canned pork and beans, chili con carne and cream soups.

It is difficult to find foods in the Western diet that do not contain fat. The result is that about 42% of all calories we consume are in the form of fat. Most health professionals believe that fat should constitute no more than 30% of the total calories consumed. Too much dietary fat contributes to obesity, a condition that can cause blood cholesterol levels to go up.

The most significant problem with fat on the Western diet, however, centers on the type of fat consumed. Basically, there are three types—saturated, polyunsaturated and monounsaturated. Saturated fat is found in animal foods, such as the visible fat on a steak, bacon drippings, lard and butter. A good rule for recognizing saturated fat is that it will solidify at refrigerator temperatures. It is estimated that about 44% of all fat consumed in the Western diet is saturated. What makes saturated fat a cardiac risk factor is that it tends to increase the amount of LDL cholesterol in the blood, thus contributing to the development of coronary artery blockages.

Conversely, polyunsaturated fat does not raise the LDL blood cholesterol. Indeed, it has a lowering effect. The one drawback is that polyunsaturated fat not only lowers bad LDL cholesterol, but it lowers good HDL cholesterol as well. The best examples of polyunsaturated fat are safflower oil, sunflower oil, corn oil, cottonseed oil and soybean oil. A characteristic of these vegetable oils is that they will stay liquid at refrigerator temperatures. Two vegetable oils to avoid are palm oil and coconut oil—both contain more saturated fat than lard.

Another good source of polyunsaturated fat is fish. Omega 3, an ingredient of fish oil, has been shown to protect against coronary heart disease. According to the *New England Journal of Medicine*, eating ''as little as two fish dishes a week may cut the risk of dying from heart attack in half.'' Fish with high fat content include salmon, mackerel, herring, fresh tuna, whitefish and lake trout.

Olive oil is the best example of monounsaturated fat. In the past, olive oil was seen as neutral; that is, it was neither helpful nor harmful to cardiac health. New studies, however, show it to be very healthful as it will lower LDL levels but will not lower HDL levels. Thus, more and more healthy diets include olive oil in moderate amounts.

The amount and the type of fat consumed does impact blood cholesterol levels. When the total quantity of fat consumed is too high, and when the total quality of fat consumed is too saturated, then dietary fat can constitute a risk for coronary heart disease. Unfortunately, such is the condition of the Western diet. It is the prime reason why so many people are victims of coronary heart disease.

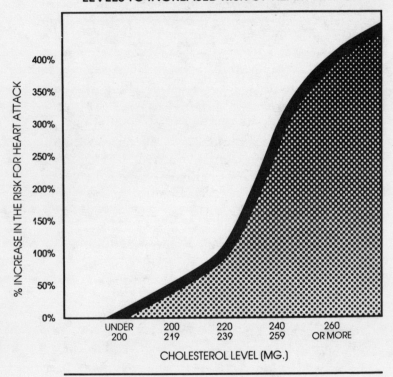

RELATIONSHIP OF BLOOD CHOLESTEROL
LEVELS TO INCREASED RISK OF HEART ATTACK

SOURCE: AMERICAN HEART ASSOCIATION POOLING PROJECT

SALT

It is dinnertime, and throughout the country people sit with family and friends to enjoy a meal together. Somewhere between the grace and the first forkful of foods comes the inevitable hallmark phrase of table conversation: "Please pass the salt"!

For most people, salt constitutes a basic dietary element. But recently many people have begun to question the amount of salt consumed on the typical modern diet. The reason? Excessive salt intake has been linked to high blood pressure (hypertension), stroke, kidney and thyroid disease, and edema. Indeed, in the U.S. the Surgeon General and the U.S. Senate's Select Committee on Nutrition have concluded studies and have issued separate reports advising Americans to restrict their salt consumption. Food columnist Craig Clairborne, himself a victim of high blood pressure, has stated that, "They should label salt, just as they do cigarettes, saying that it is injurious to your health."

What Is the Problem?

The warnings issued about salt are very serious. In order to understand the health risks associated with excessive salt consumption, it is first necessary to distinguish sodium from salt. Salt, or sodium chloride, is a combination of two minerals: sodium, a metal; and chlorine, a gas. Approximately 40% of salt is sodium. Thus, a diet which is high in salt is also a diet which is high in sodium. It is the sodium content of foods in the modern diet which constitutes a health issue.

Sodium, which is essential to life, displays both positive and negative characteristics. On the positive side, it is the chief regulator of the fluid balance of the body. The tissues in the human body must constantly be bathed in a saline solution. The correct ratio of sodium-to-water in this body fluid is critical to proper metabolic functioning.

Sodium regulates that balance by triggering a thirst sensation when body fluid is too low or sodium content is too high. For example, when a person loses fluid by sweating, the ratio of sodium-to-water is increased, causing that person to become thirsty. By drinking liquids to satisfy his thirst, he is also replacing the fluid necessary to restore the proper fluid balance. This relationship of excess sodium to thirst has long been understood by bartenders who offer free salted peanuts or popcorn to their patrons.

When the concentration of sodium in the body is constantly high, as it often is as a result of the high-salt modern diet, the fluid balance mechanism can be perverted to produce negative health results. A characteristic of sodium is that it holds water. When the body contains too much sodium and consequently too much water, the excess is eliminated through the kidneys.

Should this happen occasionally, it generally poses no health problem. But when the kidneys are required to work constantly over a long period of time to eliminate excessive sodium and water, they become overworked and are placed under great strain. Many times they simply become unable to perform at the required level of elimination, and kidney damage or failure results.

Excessive amounts of sodium and water in the blood vessels also tax the heart by increasing the volume of blood to be circulated. When this happens, the heart is required to pump harder and to create more pressure in order to move the additional pounds of fluid in the bloodsteam. At the same time sodium causes the small blood vessels to constrict, thereby increasing resistance to blood flow. The heart is forced to respond by further increasing blood pressure, which is a significant strain on the heart muscle.

Hypertension, or high blood pressure, is the most serious health consequence of excessive sodium intake. Like atherosclerosis, the disease makes a silent progression. Blood pressure may be increased year after year with no overt symptoms of any health problem. Then quite suddenly, usually in middle age, the disease appears. But by this time it is usually too late to repair the damage done to the heart, blood vessels and kidneys. Chronic illness and death often occur.

The causes of hypertension are not fully understood. Many factors, such as weight, age, stress, genetics and diet, are thought to contribute to it. Although it is difficult to prove a direct cause and effect relationship between salt and hypertension, numerous studies have established that a clear link does exist between a high-salt diet and the incidence of hypertension. These studies have shown that in low-salt cultures, such as New Guinea and parts of Brazil, high blood pressure is virtually non-existent and blood pressure does not rise steadily with age. In high-salt cultures, such as Japan and the United States, high blood pressure is rampant.

In a study conducted in the Solomon Islands by Dr. Lot Page of Harvard, six primitive tribes were studied. All six exhibited a common lifestyle with one notable exception: three tribes ate a high-salt diet. It was only in the tribes which ate such a diet that incidence of high blood pressure could be found. In Japan, where salt consumption is three to six times that of the West, areas can be found where over 40% of the adult population suffers from serious high blood pressure. It is that country's leading cause of death.

Not everyone with an excessive sodium intake is susceptible to the disease. In many people the excess is promptly excreted no matter how high the intake. But in a significant proportion of people there exists a genetic predispositioin to hypertension. For these people a diet high in salt, and consequently high in sodium, can increase the risk of hypertension and of heart disease. No procedure exists which identifies with certainty those people who have the genetic weak-link. Consequently, a person with a sodium-rich diet is playing Russian roulette with his health.

Salt Is Found Everywhere

Salt is the major source of sodium for most people. Where does all the salt in our diet come from? About 15% comes from natural sources such as meat, fish, dairy products, vegetables and drinking water. Another 35% is the result of table salt used as a condiment and a cooking spice. But the remaining 50%, the largest source, comes from processed foods found in the modern diet.

Salt and other sodium products are used by food manufacturers as a curative for fish and meats; as a brine agent for pickles, olives and sauerkraut; as a levening agent in bread and crackers; and as a fermentation control agent in cheese. The result has been to make foods which are low in sodium in a natural state into high-sodium foods in a processed state. A 5.5 ounce potato, for example, contains just 5 milligrams of sodium. But processed as potato chips, it contains 1562 milligrams. A tomato contains 14 milligrams of sodium. But processed into tomato sauce, one

46

cup contains 1498. One-half a chicken breast has 69 milligrams of sodium; a fast food chicken dinner contains 2243.

Why do processed foods contain so much salt and sodium? There are many answers beyond food preservation. One is found in economics. Salt is an inexpensive filler which adds weight and substance to processed foods. In addition, because food processing often removes the natural flavor of the food, salt is added as a flavoring substance to provide the product with some semblance of recognizable taste, thereby masking the blandness of the product. It is this salty taste which today's consumer has been conditioned to accept. And finally, the fact that salt can be addictive has not been lost on food processors.

There is no natural affinity for the taste of salt. We are not born with such a craving. The preference for a salty taste is an acquired one. The more salt eaten, the more impervious the taste buds become, and the more salt is necessary to produce a "too salty" taste. By maintaining a high level of salt in their products, many food processors have insured that their foods will be purchased not for reasons of nutrition, but for reasons of taste. From a profit standpoint, the heavy use of salt as a food additive can be justified. From a health standpoint, it cannot.

SUGAR

Excessive sugar intake has been characterized as one of the major health hazards of the modern diet. It is a contributing factor to tooth decay, obesity and diabetes. And according to many cardiac experts such as Dr. John W. Farquhar, excessive sugar constitutes a risk for coronary heart disease as well. Despite evidence of its detrimental effect upon good health, people continue their love affair with sweet taste.

Much of this sugar is consumed in the form of sweets and soft drinks, but the main source of sugar is processed foods: canned fruits, soups, gravies, cereals, salad dressings and ketchup are some of the foods in which sugar is a hidden principal ingredient. Dr. John Yudkin of London University, long a critic of sugar as a food additive, states that "if only a fraction of what is already known about the effects of sugar were to be revealed in relation to any other material used as a food additive, that material would promptly be banned."

Two Types of Sugar

An appreciation of the potential health problems associated with excessive sugar intake requires an understanding of the two types of sugar consumed. The first type is the sugar contained in fruits, berries, dairy products, grains, vegetables and other unprocessed foods. It is called "natural sugar" since it is an inherent part of the food itself. The second type of sugar is that which is added to processed foods, such as canned fruits, or that which is used as a condiment, such as table sugar sprinkled on breakfast cereal. This sugar is called "concentrated sugar". It is manufactured to produce a super-sweetness not found in natural sugar. Concentrated sugars include granulated table sugar (sucrose), brown sugar, powdered sugar, unrefined sugar and pale brown granulated invert sugar.

Both types of sugar produce energy at the rate of 4 calories per gram. In this respect it can be said that "sugar is sugar". But very significant differences appear when nutrition and caloric density of the two sugars are considered. Nutritionally, foods which contain natural sugar also contain protein, vitamins, minerals and fiber. When strawberries are consumed for their sweet taste, vital nutrients in the fruit are also supplied to the body.

Foods high in concentrated sugar, on the other hand, are often totally devoid of nutritional value. When a piece of chocolate cake is eaten for its sweet taste, it produces nothing but pure calories for the body. For this reason, foods which contain natural sugar are preferable to foods which contain concentrated sugar as an additive.

The second difference concerns caloric density, the amount of calories supplied in ratio to the bulk of the food. A food with high bulk and low calories, such as cantaloupe, has low caloric density. A food with low bulk and high calories, such as a sweet, has high caloric density.

The caloric density of foods is important because the body requires a balance between calories consumed and calories burned. When more calories are consumed than burned, the excess calories are converted into fat and stored. It does not matter what is the source of the calories — fat, protein or carbohydrate. As long as more calories are consumed than are used up, body fat will be produced.

Foods containing natural sugar generally demonstrate a low caloric density. A great many strawberries at 55 calories per cup, for example, would have to be consumed before excess body fat would be created. The chances are that because of the bulk of the food, a person would feel full before consuming too many calories.

It is not the same with foods containing concentrated sugar. These foods are generally high in caloric density. A 4-ounce milk chocolate candy bar, for example, contains 600 calories. Because this food lacks bulk, several candy bars, representing hundreds of calories, could be consumed before a person felt full. Foods containing concentrated sugar often allow a person to simultaneously occupy two opposing dietary extremes: to be overfed and to be hungry.

What Is the Problem?

A diet high in sugar represents many dangers for the heart. The first is obesity, the storage of excessive amounts of body fat, a condition that places tremendous strain upon the heart and the circulatory system. Obesity can cause the heart to be overworked in its attempt to circulate blood to the excess fat, and can promote elevated blood cholesterol. Permanent damage to the cardiac muscle can result.

The second danger is that foods rich in concentrated sugar can displace more nutritionally valuable foods in the diet. What is often perceived as a craving for sugar may simply be a hunger pang. But instead of appeasing the hunger with nutritional foods, many people satisfy their hunger with foods containing concentrated sugar — a cookie, a doughnut, or a piece of pie. While these foods may satisfy, they are a poor substitute for a balanced meal. In this situation the heart is robbed of needed nutrients.

Finally, sugar has been shown to raise triglycerides. Clinical studies in Yemen, South Africa, Japan, East Africa and the United States have concluded that concentrated sugar acts to increase triglycerides in certain people and can increase their risk of coronary heart disease.

50

The Sweet Tooth Syndrome

Why do we eat sweet foods? The fact is that man genuinely has a "sweet tooth". A preference for sweet taste has been demonstrated throughout history. Even the Bible described the Promised Land as "flowing with milk and honey." No other animal (with the possible exception of cats) demonstrates such an inclination. But the craving in man is sufficiently strong to affect his dietary decisions.

Foods containing natural sugar had been used to satisfy the sweet craving until the time of the Industrial Revolution. Fruits and berries not only were sweet, they were also important nutritionally to a proper diet. With the advent of the sugar refining process around 1800, man began to gravitate toward foods which contained concentrated sugar. Industrialization produced a more civilized lifestyle for many people, including dietary changes which called for sweeter and richer foods as a symbol of affluence and status. Cream, butter and refined sugar became popular. Fruits and berries were replaced by pastry, cakes and candies.

Very little concentrated sugar was consumed in the early 1800s — only about two pounds per person annually. Refined sugar was an expensive commodity and not everyone could afford it. But a more important reason was one of taste. The sweet tooth of 1800 could be satisfied on only two pounds of sugar a year.

Advances in technology reduced the cost of producing refined sugar and by the late 1800s it was available to the entire population.

As people continued to increase sugar consumption, the amount of sugar needed to satisfy the sweet tooth also increased. The more sugar eaten, the more sugar desired.

51

It took thirty-five times the amount of sugar in 1910 than it did in 1800 to meet the sweet craving.

The development of the processed food and beverage industry in the 20th century has caused the consumption of refined sugar and other sugar concentrates to skyrocket. Sugar has replaced salt as the most popular food additive.

According to Dr. John Yudkin and other experts, sugar is addictive. The more of it contained in the diet, the more of it that is needed to satisfy the sweet tooth craving. The result is a diet which contains more sugar intake in a single week than our forefathers consumed in an entire year. The health consequences have been disastrous for us.

MYTHS OF THE MODERN DIET

During the research process I became convinced of two things: 1. *that diet pattern does have an impact upon cardiac health,* and 2. *that my diet pattern – the contemporary diet – was too full of fat, cholesterol, salt, sugar and total calories.* The need to change the way I ate was evident.

Nevertheless, to do so was a cultural shock. For 32 years I had eaten the classic "healthy" meat and milk diet, based on the premise that the more of these products you consumed, the better for you. So my Mother dutifully prepared meals rich in red meat and dairy products, and I dutifully consumed them. After all, we thought, fortified with quantities of protein and calcium, I would grow straight and strong, have sparkling teeth, and leap tall buildings in a single bound.

Nothing was ever said about coronary heart disease. Somehow the information linking diet to atherosclerosis fell through the cracks. As a result, it was not until my coronary surgery that I came to understand many of the shortcomings of my "healthy" diet. A number of these have become solidified in our culture as myths.

Myth Number 1: Eat Lots of Red Meat

There is no argument that red meat is an important source of protein. That is an indisputable fact. The fallacy concerns the amount of protein needed for good health. And the amount of saturated fat consumed with the protein.

Large quantities of red meat can provide more protein than is needed each day for good health. The body cannot always utilize excessive protein and in some instances it may even cause health problems.

The most significant problem, however, is that making animal food the principal source of protein overloads the diet with saturated fat. When red meat is consumed for protein, fat is consumed as well. Generally, the fat content of red meat is many times more than the protein content. In truth, red meat consumption can be diminished drastically without neglecting protein needs.

Myth Number 2: Eat and Drink Lots of Dairy Products.

Whole milk dairy products also constituted a large percentage of my pre-surgery diet. I drank 2-4 glasses of milk each day, and ate butter, cheese, and ice cream. These foods provided me with calcium for the development and maintenance of strong bones and teeth. But the same problem existed here as with red meat: the consumption level of dairy products far outstripped the needs of my body for calcium, resulting in a high intake of saturated butterfat as well.

It was not the nutrition of the food which was in question. It was the quantity of the food seen as necessary to provide calcium benefit. We can obtain what we need each day from just 3½ ounces of low-fat cheese or three cups of skim milk. A number of vegetables, notably spinach, also are rich in calcium. The great amount of dairy products in my diet not only produced excess calcium but also were a significant source of saturated fat.

Myth Number 3: Start Each Day with a High-Protein Breakfast

How many times had I heard this message in the course of my life? Each time the pitch would advocate the classic high-protein breakfast: eggs, ham, bacon and sausage; toast with butter; cereal with whole milk or half-and-half; juice; and coffee. It is indeniable that this breakfast is a high-protein meal. But it constitutes a high-fat meal as well. The promotion of the protein content exclusively is a little like saying that Pill "X" will clear your sinuses without revealing a side effect that will cause your nose to fall off!

Let's examine this high-protein breakfast. The juice is wholesome, as may be the cereal (unless it is sugared). But the milk used on the cereal and in the coffee and the butter on the toast are high in saturated butterfat. The eggs are rich in cholesterol, especially when cooked in butter or fat. And the breakfast meats could easily be over 75% in fat content.

54

This might be a high-protein breakfast, but it is also a breakfast that is too rich in saturated fat to be healthful. It took coronary surgery for me to appreciate this fact.

Myth Number 4: Fast Foods Are Nutritious and Healthful.

My guess was that this was dependent upon who was defining "nutritious". By my post-surgery standards, I find this claim to be pure bunk, aimed at unaware children and guilt-ridden parents.

It cannot be argued that fast foods and convenience foods are not tasty, for they are. No one enjoyed the taste of hamburgers, tacos, milk shakes, pizza and doughnuts more than I did. And I was not alone. It takes millions of people to spend $25 billion annually on fast foods and $10 billion on snacks — and that does not count the money spent in grocery stores for convenience foods such as frozen dinners. We are attracted to these foods because they are fast, filling, inexpensive and attractive to youngsters, and because we have learned to like the taste.

But nutritious? That is quite another thing. The amount of fat, sugar and calories — not to mention fillers, preservatives and chemicals — in these foods may overshadow any nutritional content. A McDonald's Big Mac has 570 calories and is 55% fat. These foods can be too high in saturated fat to be healthy.

Fast food processing has changed the nutritional benefit of many foods. Potatoes in the raw state, for example, can supply a large percentage of daily requirements for protein, vitamins and minerals. They are low in calories and fats, and high in desirable complex carbohydrates. But when processed as a French fry or a crisp, the raw potato

is fried in deep fat and its original nutritional
benefit is decreased. It then becomes a high-fat,
high-calorie, high-salt food.

The fast food industry, I concluded, might talk
about nutrition and food composition, but in reality they were really concerned with predictability,
cleanliness and efficiency. It was name recogni-
tion, not nutrition, which was the paramount
goal. As a fast food aficionado, I knew that they
were tasty. But as a cardiac patient, I know that
they may be neither nutritious nor healthful.

Myth Number 5: Processed Foods Are As
                 Nutritious As Natural Foods.

The same argument holds here as with fast foods.
Certainly canned, frozen, and dehydrated foods
offer some nutritional value. Some offer considerably more than others. But the additives in many
of these foods are of sufficient quantity to offset
most nutritional value. Salt and refined sugar are
the two most popular food additives. An excess of
salt in the diet can lead to high blood pressure; an
excess of sugar can lead to elevated blood fats and
obesity. In addition, many processed foods use
saturated fat in the form of butter or lard as a flavor
enhancer.

Salt, sugar, fat . . . these are dietary elements
which in excess can lead to coronary heart disease.
Not all processed foods are bad. But enough of
them contain additives that no one can simply
assume that processed foods are nutritious and
healthy.

Myth Number 6: Refined Sugar Is an Energy Food.

Every day millions of people reach for a candy bar or
soft drink for quick energy. They have been con-

vinced by the sugar industry's advertising that refined sugar is an energy food. This is simply not the case.

Confusion over the word "sugar" is what has provided the advertisers with the literary license to produce the energy myth. The term "sugar" can be applied to natural sugar, such as that found in fruit, as well as to concentrated refined sugar, which is found in candy.

The most important of the natural sugars is glucose. Food is converted into glucose, which in turn is burned by the tissues for energy. As such, glucose is always in the bloodstream, available to the tissues when needed. It is referred to as "blood sugar".

But "blood sugar" has nothing to do with refined sugar. When it is said that sugar is an energy food, what is meant is that glucose is an energy food. The sugar industry, however, has created the impression that refined sugar is what the body uses as fuel.

Myth Number 7: Salt Is a Needed Preservative.

Almost any canned, prepackaged, dried or frozen food available in the supermarket today contains salt or sodium derivatives, such as sodium benzoate, sodium nitrate or sodium glutamate, as a "necessary preservative". In fact, salt does act as a preservative; but that is not the chief reason for its addition to many processed foods. The main reason lies in the fact that many processed foods are tasteless. They are often refined to the point where no taste is left in them. So, the food processors needed to create an artificial taste that people would like. Salt creates that taste.

Salt is often referred to as a "flavor enhancer" or as a "natural seasoning". In reality, it is neither. It is a means to capitalize on the Western addiction to salty taste in order to sell more processed foods. This myth has contributed to a diet pattern which supplies about twenty times more salt than is needed each day.

Myth Number 8: It Is Natural and Acceptable To Put On Weight As You Get Older.

The average American gains one or two pounds a year after age 20. This has made them a nation of overweight people. Many adults who are 20 or 30 pounds overweight consider themselves to be normal and healthy, their weight a natural occurrence of aging.

It is not "normal" to gain weight as you get older. Weight gain is not a natural occurrence. Instead, it is a product of overconsumption of calories and under-activity in physical exercise. In many less developed, less sedentary countries, adults lose weight as they age, a product of the normal loss of heavier lean muscle mass that comes with growing older. Western people are fatter at 50 than 20 not because age and fatness go together naturally, but because the modern diet encourages us to eat too much, eat too often, and eat too many high caloric foods.

A LAST WORD

St. Thomas Aquinas, a most intelligent and scholarly person, subscribed to the thesis that all things should be done in moderation. This was for him the key to both physical and spiritual health. Fortunately for him, St. Thomas never had the opportunity to meet a twentieth century person and be confronted with a lifestyle which often reflects extremes.

One of the most significant extremes of the modern lifestyle is our diet pattern. There is so much available to our affluent society that we eat without any sense of what we are doing or why we are doing it. By eating excessive amounts of cholesterol, saturated fat, sugar, salt and total calories, we have contributed to our own demise. The epidemic proportions of coronary heart disease, obesity, high blood pressure and heart attacks in the West today are culturally induced, in part by a diet which is too extreme to be healthful.

THE REVERSIBILITY OF ATHEROSCLEROSIS

Not all the news concerning diet is bad. Recent medical research has indicated that atherosclerosis may be reversible, that coronary artery blockages could be reduced in number and size, as the result of dietary changes. This research illustrates not only that a high-fat diet is a risk factor for developing coronary heart disease, but conversely, that a low-fat diet could minimize the risks of that disease. It means that by controlling his diet, an individual could exercise some control over his cardiac future.

Among the most significant of the studies made in this area were those conducted by Dr. M.L. Armstrong. Over a 5-year period he tested a group of 30 Rhesus monkeys. All the monkeys were fed a high-fat/high-cholesterol diet during the first two years in order to determine the effect of the disease. (Neither the diet pattern nor the disease was common to the Rhesus monkey.) At the end of that time, 10 animals were examined and found to have severe atherosclerosis. Their coronary artery blockages were numerous and of significant size. This information became the baseline for further testing.

The remaining animals, whose arteries were presumed by Dr. Armstrong to be equally athero-sclerotic, were divided into two equal groups. Group 1 was placed on a low-fat/low-cholesterol diet, while Group 2 was placed on a medium-fat/low-cholesterol diet. At the end of three years, the animals were examined. The Group 1 animals were found to have arterial blockages which were 75% smaller than those found in the baseline group. The blockages in Group 2 were 35% smaller than the original group.

A significant reduction in blockages had taken place in this test as a result of dietary change. Dr. Armstrong concluded that a diet low in fat and cholesterol could be effective in reversing the buildup of coronary artery blockages.

A great deal of research is still to be done in this area for the evidence is much less conclusive in humans than in test animals. However, the initial results indicate that diet pattern may be a two-edged sword: it can work for you as well as against you. And that means that if properly managed, diet need not constitute a cardiac risk factor.

CHAPTER FOUR

THE POSITIVE DIET

"Lifestyle" is a very contemporary word. It has unique shades of meaning for different individuals, but for all of us it says much about the way in which we live and about what is important to us. How we live often dictates how we eat. Diet pattern is frequently a product of custom, habit, convenience, economics and social standing. Some families enjoy a certain special meal on Sundays or on holidays. Modern wives often utilize convenience foods to save time. Young people congregate at fast food restaurants. Those who can afford it dine on haute cuisine. And children, often responding to television advertising, beg for certain breakfast cereals.

The body, however, has no concept of lifestyle. It is a machine which needs to be fueled in order to perform. The food which is eaten provides that fuel. The body does not care about the appeasement of psychological, social and culinary appetites. It is concerned exclusively with the nutritional value of what is consumed. It is like an automobile which needs petrol to run. It cares not whether the petrol is expensive or cheap, just so long as it produces usable fuel.

I had not understood this in the past and consequently the food choices on my diet had been made for other than nutritive reasons. After my surgery, I began to realize that the decisions concerning food choices had to be based upon the results generated, rather than upon taste, preparation time or the endorsement of a superstar.

Along with this realization came an understanding of the word "diet." In my pre-surgery lifestyle, diet had a singular connotation. It was a weight reduction program, a means of shedding excess pounds rapidly by controlling the intake of calories. Only fat people were concerned with diet. Periodically they went on and off a diet, much like Toynbee's cyclical theory of history, until either the on, or more likely the off, would eventually dominate. In this context, there was no relationship between diet and health.

After researching diet as a risk factor, I understood that *a diet could be a long-term manner of eating* and *a diet pattern could generate negative or positive results.* In analyzing my diet, it was obvious that it was a "negative diet," that indeed it had produced a negative impact upon my cardiac health. What was needed, I reasoned, was a "positive diet," a diet which would be a permanent program of healthful eating.

Using the knowledge gained, I determined the important elements of such a "Positive Diet":

>It must be in tune with contemporary lifestyle.
>In order to be achievable, it must be realistic.
>It must meet psychological needs as well as physical needs.
>It must be motivated by an understanding of the importance of healthful eating.
>It must maximize the heart-healthy foods and minimize the harmful foods.

It was easy to understand and to accept the "why" of the Positive Diet. Much information testified to the fact that such a diet could be instrumental in the prevention and perhaps the reversal of coronary heart disease. The difficulty as Dr. Nagle had indicated, would be in the "how".

When I left the hospital after surgery, I was issued a standard low-cholesterol diet, really nothing more than a listing of good and bad foods. It was based on the premise that some foods were healthful and should be eaten, while others were harmful and should be avoided.

The missing link was that the standard diet did not explain how to apply the premise, how to change the eating habits of a lifetime, or how to make it work. It just said, "You better do it!" Granted, with the surgery fresh in my mind, my motivation to stay on a new diet was great. But how long, I asked myself, could I survive on carrot sticks — the Peter Rabbit approach to cardiac health — before saying, "The hell with it!" and reverting to my tasty, old, comfortable diet? Without the "how," the new diet was meaningless.

"We can only make general dietary recommendations for you," Dr. Nagle had said to me. "We can't design a diet to specifically suit your needs and your tastes, and we can't make it work for you. Many of my patients have had a strong motivation to modify their diet. Yet, the vast majority have been unable to do so with any degree of success. A number have returned to their original diet — the same diet which had contributed to their cardiac problem in the first place. Why? Because without a realistic, step-by-step program to follow, the patient never understands how a new diet can be accomplished. Generally, after a few months of trying, the cardiac patient gives up in frustration."

As I experimented over the months to develop a new diet, his words became even more meaningful to me. Frustration plagued me. Progress was elusive. Without a tested plan to follow, I was never quite sure whether or not my new diet was working. The author Graham Greene had once said that there was no black and white but only shades of gray. And that was how the Positive Diet initially appeared to me: in ellusive, chiaroscura form.

Gradually, however, it emerged from the gray and took on clarity in the light. After more than a year of work, it existed not just in theory, but in reality, and in the process it became an integral, permanent part of my lifestyle. I finally understood not only why I had made the dietary change, but how I made it as well.

The Positive Diet

Before the Positive Diet can be successful, one needs to understand its basic principles and tools. He also needs to recognize the underlying premise for the practice of the diet:
>That each individual is responsible for his own health.
>That a decision to eat "positively" must include an understanding of diet as a cardiac risk factor.
>That a firm commitment must be made to make the Positive Diet a permanent diet pattern.

THE BASIC PRINCIPLES

The fundamental cardiac risk involved with the contemporary Western diet concerns excesses. While dietary deficiencies are still the major problem in many areas of the world, in the West the biggest problem is the inordinate amount of fat, cholesterol, sugar, salt and total calories consumed. Recognizing this fact, the basic principles of the Positive Diet are designed to reduce or to eliminate certain harmful foods. The four basic principles are as follows:

1. *Reduce the intake of animal fat and cholesterol.* As has been illustrated in numerous medical studies and field tests, a direct and causal relationship exists between the intake of animal fat and cholesterol, the elevation of blood cholesterol levels, and the development of coronary heart disease. While a diet high in fat and cholesterol may only be one of a number of factors which ultimately cause the disease, it clearly is a factor.

2. *Reduce the intake of butterfat.* Butterfat, which is a saturated fat, contributes to cardiac problems in the same way as does animal fat by promoting high blood cholesterol.

3. *Reduce the intake of salt.* Excess salt in the diet contributes to the development of hypertension, hardening of the arteries, and coronary heart disease.

4. *Reduce the intake of refined sugar.* Not only has sugar displaced needed nutritive foods in the diet, but it has contributed to obesity and to high blood fat levels, both of which constitute significant risks for coronary heart disease.

THE BASIC TOOLS

The four basic principles, concerned with reduction, must be combined with meal planning and creative substitution for permanent change to take place. Meal planning and creative substitution — called the basic tools of the Positive Diet — allow for the creation of new healthful meals. They are dedicated to the belief that if satisfaction can be found in the foods which should be eaten, then there will not be the inclination for the foods which should not be eaten.

Meal Planning

The meal plan is the first step to success and is critical to the practice of the Positive Diet. A meal plan defines in advance how to successfully stay on the diet. The Positive Diet meal plan is the selection of which foods to eat over a designated period of time, usually one to three weeks. By listing the foods for each meal ahead of time, the meal plan can ensure the inclusion of nutritious foods and the exclusion of harmful foods. The meal plan minimizes the meals which are left to chance. It prevents an individual from approaching a mealtime only to ask himself, "What do I do now?"

Meal planning was essential to my success with the Positive Diet. I began the planning process by dividing the week into 21 meals. Using the basic principles as a guide, I began to plan a meal schedule which either reduced or eliminated harmful foods. On my pre-surgery diet, for example, I frequently ate red meat. To ensure that the fat and cholesterol content of my meals would be drastically reduced, I charted a meal plan for the Positive Diet that reduced red meat to just four meals per week.

Another advantage to using a meal plan is that it allows for certain favorite, but not-so-healthy foods to be phased out gradually, rather than eliminated abruptly. Abrupt elimination can cause a feeling of being unjustly deprived and result in resentment.

For example, abruptly giving up a daily breakfast of bacon and eggs could be very discouraging. All of the fat and cholesterol arguments in the world might not work. With meal planning, however, one could begin to practise the Positive Diet by reducing the number of times bacon and eggs were eaten for breakfast. Further reductions and possible elimination could come in future meal plans. The result not only would be an immediate reduction in fat and cholesterol, but also a more ready acceptance of the Positive Diet as a permanent diet pattern.

An additional reason for using a meal plan is to involve all members of the family in the act of planning. Eating is a family affair, and good cardiac health is the business of the entire family. When everyone in the family understands why the Positive Diet is necessary and provides input as to what should be eaten, there generally is more cooperation.

In our family, we decided together what meals to eat during the coming week. Even our youngest child had his say. Total family participation reduced the number of surprises at meals and led to a firmer commitment by each person to practise the Positive Diet. It resulted in a sharing of responsibility, pride and support which helped to keep everyone eating healthfully. Even the children could understand that we were eating right not just for Daddy's heart, but for their own hearts as well.

Meal planning does take some work to be successful. In the beginning I found our meal plans to be restrictive and repetitive. This was to be expected — after all, I was attempting to change the dietary habits of a lifetime. After a while we developed a larger selection of tested menus and recipes, which gave me more culinary choices.

Today, with the Positive Diet an integral part

of our family lifestyle, meal planning has become more a guideline and less a rigid plan. It has become second nature to the extent that a formal meal plan is no longer necessary. However, had meal planning not been used at the beginning of the diet, I do not believe that success would have been possible.

There are sample meal plans provided in this book. It is not necessary to use my meal plans to practice the Positive Diet successfully; but it is necessary to use a meal plan.

Creative Substitution

Creative substitution is the process of substituting healthful foods and ingredients for harmful ones while still preserving the appeal and the taste of the food. It is one thing to remove harmful foods from the diet. It is quite another to fill the void with alternative foods which are nutritive, tasty, easily prepared, and acceptable to the Western palate.

The long term challenge is to produce satisfying meals made up of healthful foods, so that harmful foods will not be missed. Creative substitution is a necessary tool to effect permanent dietary change. Fortunately, it is easily done. It is an art, and like any other art it can be perfected over time.

I knew when I began the Positive Diet that creative substitution would be essential to its success. While there was a legitimate place in my diet for raw carrots and unmilled grain, without the creative use of these foods in acceptable recipes such a diet was doomed. For that reason, I spent time during the development period talking with physicians, nutritionists and, most importantly, other cardiac patients about the problem of permanent acceptability of a heart-healthy diet.

Their comments coincided with my own experience and led to this conclusion: in order for a healthy diet to become permanent, it must offer foods which are acceptable to the Western palate. This meant that my meals had to be made more healthy, rather than eliminated. And it meant that creative substitution was of extreme importance in accomplishing such a change.

For example, saturated animal fats, often used in Western cooking, are unhealthy. Fish oil is a healthy alternative, but is not familiar to our tastes. For that reason, it is an unrealistic substitution despite its healthful qualities. Safflower oil would be a more acceptable substitute. Thus, in creating the menus and the recipes for the Positive Diet we paid as much attention to Western taste as to healthfulness.

The process of creative substitution took two forms. The first was a simple "one-for-one" exchange of heart-healthy food for less healthful food. Barbecued or broiled salmon, for example, replaced beefsteak. Since salmon is lower in fat and cholesterol, it is a good one-for-one substitution. Many other harmful foods were easy to replace: skim milk for whole milk; egg substitute for whole eggs; chicken sandwiches for pastrami sandwiches; unsalted peanuts for salted peanuts; and fruit juice for soft drinks. Even for those new to the Positive Diet, this form of creative substitution is an easy one to learn, especially when used in conjunction with a meal plan.

The second form of creative substitution was more difficult to master, but was also fundamental to the success of the diet. This form involves the substitution of healthful ingredients for harmful items in a recipe. It allows a meal normally unacceptable to a heart-healthy diet to become acceptable by removing the harmful ingredients and substituting more healthful ingredients. For example, in beef stroganoff, fat-rich sour cream and commercially prepared cream of chicken soup were replaced by non-fat yogurt and homemade chicken broth. In effect, the form and the taste of the Western diet pattern can be preserved, while the quality can be drastically changed for the better.

Another form of creative substitution is to alter the cooking method. For example, commercially prepared, fat-laden French fries are artery blockers. But heart-healthy French fries can be made by substituting unsaturated liquid vegetable oil for animal fat and by using oven-baking in place of deep fat frying. And chocolate cake can include safflower oil in place of butter and shortening and cocoa powder in place of baking chocolate.

Creative substitution with ingredients takes time and practice to develop, but with proficiency comes an increasing ability to turn negative diet meals into Positive Diet meals. When that happens, the best of both worlds is gained.

APPLYING THE BASIC PRINCIPLES AND THE BASIC TOOLS

After I understood why adherence to the Positive Diet was critical for me, I began to deal with the real question: how to make it work? Could I produce meals which were tasty and healthful? Would too much time be spent in cooking? Would the meals be expensive? Was the Positive Diet a practical one?

My decision was to disregard the "woulds"

and the "shoulds," and to direct my attention to just getting started, but to do so in an orderly fashion. I did not believe that even with an understanding of diet and motivation to change, I could totally reverse a 32-year-old behavior pattern instantly.

Instead of attempting complete dietary control by simultaneously adopting all four basic principles, I decided to work with one at a time. Start with the first basic principle, I reasoned, get it firmly established in my diet pattern, then move on to the second. When that one was in place, go to the third, and so on. By taking the time to concentrate on specific pieces of the program, I could make steady progress. This method would be far preferable to the quick, but potentially short-lived adoption of all the basic principles simultaneously.

And so I began.

CHAPTER FIVE

IMPLEMENTING THE POSITIVE DIET

The practical application of the Positive Diet involves two steps. The first is to analyze diet pattern and identify the sources of fat, cholesterol, salt and sugar. The second is to design and implement specific actions to reduce these unhealthy elements.

REDUCING FAT AND CHOLESTEROL

The first basic principle, the reduction of fat and cholesterol, is one of the most important.

Step Number 1: Identification of Fat and Cholesterol Sources

Red meat was the largest single source of fat and cholesterol on my pre-surgery diet. I ate ham, sausage or bacon for breakfast; bologna sandwiches, salami sandwiches, hot dogs, or fast food hamburgers for lunch; steaks, chops, roasts, or meat loaf for dinner.

I looked at food composition tables and they highlighted the high-protein myth of the Western diet. If every 100 calories from sirloin steak produces 76 calories of fat and just 24 calories of protein, there is no reasonable way this food can be classified as "high-protein" without also being classified as "high-fat." The same holds true for other meat products.

Fats and oils were also a major source of fat on my diet. Hydrogenated margarine, even when made from unsaturated vegetable oil, is about 99% fat. I used it on toast, rolls, and bread. It was also used in sauces, baking and frying. Salad dressings, such as Blue Cheese, Thousand Island and Roquefort, are about 75% fat. Palm oil and coconut oil, both of which are rich in saturated fat, are included in most crackers, convenience foods and non-dairy substitutes.

The list did not stop there. Gravies and sauces made from meat drippings were high in saturated fat, as were fast foods. Ten French fries, about 2 ounces, contain 156 calories. That in itself is frightening. But over 40% of those calories are derived from fat. And most canned, pre-mixed, frozen or dehydrated convenience foods use animal fat. Of the fat contained in pork and beans, for example, 40% is saturated; of that in a frozen meat loaf dinner, 35% is saturated; and of that in a chocolate cake mix, 37% is saturated.

The sources of cholesterol were the next aspect of my diet to be analyzed. Any food which comes from an animal contains cholesterol. However, certain foods contain more than others, and these cholesterol-rich foods had to be identified and restricted or eliminated if I were to reduce my intake to below 300 mg. a day.

The red meats on my diet, already damned for being high in saturated fat, contained much cholesterol. Just 12 ounces of beef, pork, lamb or veal could put me over the 300 mg. level. Two average frankfurters could constitute almost one-fifth of that level, and a single salami sandwich could comprise over one-third. Organ meats, such as liver, kidney or sweetbreads, also had too much cholesterol to remain on my diet. A 4-oz. portion of liver, for example, contains 500 mg. of cholesterol.

Animal fats used in cooking also contributed

to my cholesterol level, as did eggs. One large egg (1.8 oz.) contains 251 mg. of cholesterol. With two eggs for breakfast, I could almost double the daily recommended guideline.

Step Number 2: Reduction of Fat and Cholesterol

Dinner was the starting point for the practice of the Positive Diet. It was selected because it was the most easily controlled meal in our family schedule, it was regularly eaten at home, a variety of foods were heart-healthy as dinner fare, and normally more preparation time was available than for other meals. My pre-surgery diet had included red meat at five or six dinners in the course of a week. My initial action was to develop a meal plan which would limit red meat dinners to no more than three per week, or about a 50% reduction from my old diet.

Further steps were also taken with these red meat dinners to reduce the amount of fat and cholesterol consumed. They were as follows:

▶ Reduce meat portions in size and increase complex carbohydrates (vegetables, fruit, grains and legumes.)
▶ Use only lean-grade meat and trim it of all visible fat before cooking.
▶ Broil, roast, bake or barbecue meats as these methods allow the fat to drip away during cooking.
▶ Cook meat to medium or to well-done to maximize the fat loss during cooking.
▶ Avoid frying foods in hydrogenated margarine or animal fats; instead use chicken or beef broth, wine, water, flavored vinegars, or use a non-stick pan.

▶Always de-fat meat drippings and broths by refrigeration (the fat coagulates and can be skimmed and discarded) before using in gravies or sauces.

▶Avoid packaged, canned or frozen meat dishes as their fat content cannot be controlled.

▶Be careful of restaurant foods, especially fast foods, as their fat content cannot be controlled.

For three nights I could eat red meat which, with the exception of portion size and cooking method, was close to those meals on my old diet. But what about the other four nights?

The answer was found in simple one-for-one substitutions using poultry and seafood. Skinless, white poultry is only about 20% fat. Only 19% of the calories in trout are fat, and only 6% of those in water-packed tuna are fat. In addition, poultry and seafood, with the exception of shrimp, are generally lower in cholesterol than is red meat. (Although shrimp is high in cholesterol, many medical professionals now feel that the healthful benefits of fish oil allow shrimp to be eaten on a moderate basis.) A 3½ oz. serving of cooked trout, halibut or chicken, for example, yields cholesterol values respectively of 55 mg., 60 mg., and 79 mg. Four ounces of cod contain just 57 mg. and 3 oz. of tuna just 54 mg. of cholesterol. Four ounces of sirloin steak, by comparison, contain 107 mg. of cholesterol.

One-for-one substitutions were effective in limiting fat and cholesterol. We also took other steps to ensure that the substitutions would be as low-fat and low-cholesterol as possible. These steps were:

▶Reduce poultry and seafood portions in size. Although lower in cholesterol than red meat, poultry and seafood are still sources of cholesterol.

▶Always cook poultry without the skin so that the fat in the skin does not drip into the meat.

▶Select the white meat of the chicken or turkey, rather than the dark meat, as the white is lower in cholesterol.

▶Broil, roast, bake, steam, poach or barbecue poultry and seafood as these methods allow the fat to drip away during cooking.

▶Use wine, herbs, lemon juice or flavored vinegars, rather than margarine, oils and sauces, to flavor poultry and seafood dishes.

▶Use shellfish high in cholesterol (such as shrimp) moderately.

▶Avoid packaged, canned or frozen poultry and seafood dishes.

▶When ordering seafood and poultry in restaurants, avoid any sauces and gravies, and select only heart-healthy cooking methods.

The one-for-one substitutions were easily made. Soon barbecued chicken replaced barbecued steak, baked salmon replaced roast beef, a a tuna sandwich replaced a hamburger. Before long, I was ready to substitute ingredients.

Our goal was to preserve the taste of my old diet while stripping the dishes of their not-so-healthy elements. Chili made with mince, for example, had always been a favorite of mine. But it was also a high-fat meal. So, I began to make it using chicken rather than beef. The result? A delicious, heart-healthy chili. The same was true of cioppino. By substituting liquid safflower oil or olive oil for butter or margarine in the recipe, cioppino could be adapted to the Positive Diet. Through creative substitution, it was possible to make low-fat food taste good.

Soon the two-week dinner meal plan was complete. The red meat substitutes on this plan were not the tasteless meals of a bland diet. They easily kept me from craving red meat or feeling deprived. I was too busy eating savory, wholesome foods to be concerned with those foods no longer on my diet. In addition, the meal plan was economical. Monday's roast chicken produced the stock for Friday's soup. Roast beef yielded French Dip sandwiches. The vegetable stir-fry used vegetables left over from earlier meals. And the cioppino was a product of the sole and clam dinners.

After a few months I began to prefer this dinner pattern to that of my old meat-rich diet. Soon I was able to adjust red meat dinners downward to 2 per week without any problem. I was eating better and was more satisfied, yet the saturated fat and cholesterol were reduced. Thanks to meal planning and creative substitution, I had the best of both worlds.

Other refinements were made to further reduce fat and cholesterol. They were as follows:

▶Use fresh vegetables whenever possible. If it is necessary to use canned or frozen, read the label to ensure that the product does not contain saturated fat, such as lard, bacon fat, palm oil or coconut oil. If a label lists "vegetable fat" without revealing the specific source, assume that it is palm oil or coconut oil and do not purchase the product.

▶Use only those salad dressings made from olive oil or from an unsaturated vegetable oil (safflower, corn, cottonseed, sesame, soybean and sunflower). Use homemade rather than commercial salad dressings for maximum control over the oil, salt, sugar and preservatives. Avoid dressings made with cheese. Serve dressings on the side as only 1 tablespoon can be 75 to 100 calories.

▶Use soft tub-type margarine made from an unsaturated liquid vegetable oil in place of hydrogenated stick margarine. Again, label reading is the key. To be acceptable, the label must list liquid vegetable oil as the first ingredient and show that the product contains twice the amount of unsaturated as saturated fat.

►Reduce the amount of margarine used on breads. Even tub margarine made from an unsaturated vegetable oil is 99% fat and contains 95 calories per tablespoon. Eliminate margarine as a sauce for vegetables, rice and potatoes; instead use herbs, spices, wine, lemon juice or flavored vinegars.

►Avoid commercial bakery products and desserts that are high in saturated fat and calories.

►Increase the amount of complex carbohydrates (such as rice, beans, pasta) to satisfy in a low-fat manner and reduce the portion size of the entrée.

Lunch. After practising the Positive Diet for about two months, dinner was under control. Meal planning and creative substitution were being utilized regularly; fat and cholesterol were being reduced; and I was satisfied physically and psychologically with my meals. I then began to apply the first basic principle at lunch.

Lunch had always posed a fat and cholesterol problem. This was especially true during the weekdays, when time often dictated a fast food lunch. But I had not realized how much fat was consumed in these lunches.

Fat Content of Fast Foods

Fast Food	Calories	% of Calories from Fat
Big Mac (McDonald's)	550	53%
Quarter Pounder/with cheese (McDonald's)	518	51%
Three Piece Dinner (Kentucky Fried Chicken)		
Original	830	47%
Crispy	1070	52%
French Fries (McDonald's)	211	47%

Source: Reprinted from *Diabetes Forecast* with permission. Copyright 1979 by the American Diabetes Association, Inc.

79

It became obvious that fast foods, as well as fatty luncheon meats such as salami or bologna, had to be eliminated. This was not easy. In fact, I found the institution of the Positive Diet at lunch to be more difficult than it had been at dinner. There was no intelligent alternative but to make it work; but eating, I soon found out, was not always a matter of intellect. It was more often a matter of emotion.

Strawmen arguments were raised in my mind about why eating Positive Diet lunches were impossible: "I was in a hurry"; "I was with friends and they chose the restaurant"; "It would have been embarassing to complain about the buttersauce"; or my favorite, "I work hard and I deserve a salami sandwich!" Lunch became a battleground as to which would control my diet, intellect or emotion.

Finally, after much tribulation, common sense won. Sticking to the diet was not only a matter of rational choice, it was also a matter of having the will and the determination to do what I knew was right. I had to control my diet, not let it control me, if I were to have any say in my cardiac destiny.

I accepted the necessity of having to pack a lunch, but I did not like it. I had never taken my lunch to work in the past. I told myself that was because I liked to eat out. But the real problem was not my affinity for restaurant lunches . . . it was my ego. I was really concerned with whether or not I would continue to be viewed as a "successful executive" by my business peers if I carried a sandwich box. What would people say?

Ridiculous as this seems in retrospect, at the time the problem was real for me. After a while, I concluded that my identity problem was secondary to my coronary problem. At this early state of the Positive Diet, restaurant lunches meant no control, and no control meant no diet. Bringing my lunch from home was the only viable alternative.

Since salads were somewhat cumbersome, the meal plan was designed around sandwiches, fresh fruit, and crisp raw vegetables. I knew what I should not have: fast foods and fatty luncheon meats. I also decided to eat sandwiches containing red meat no more than once a week.

I used creative substitution to plan lunches for the remaining four days. Many of these lunches were a product of previous dinners. Roast turkey breast for a Monday dinner yielded sliced turkey sandwiches for a Wednesday lunch. Chicken dinner leftovers became a chicken sandwich for lunch. I also rediscovered two old favorites: water-packed tuna and natural peanut butter.

Breads became very important. They needed to be tasty and filling, and provide variety, as well as to meet the low-fat standards of the diet. Reading labels helped me find many acceptable choices such as certain brands of sourdough, rye, French, pumpernickel, Armenian, whole wheat, bran wheat and whole grain. Lettuce, tomtoes, onions, sprouts, almonds and water chestnuts were great garnishes and provided me with needed raw vegetables. Safflower mayonnaise, either commercial or home-made, was an acceptable spread. And I always packed fresh fruit for dessert. Soon my two-week meal plan was complete.

Week 1   Lunches

Monday	Tuna with lettuce, tomato, onion, sprouts and water chestnuts on whole wheat bread; Granny Smith apple.
Tuesday	Sliced roast turkey with lettuce, tomato and sprouts on thick crust French bread; grapes.
Wednesday	Sliced cold roast beef with tomato and onion on sour-dough roll; tangerine.
Thursday	Thinly sliced low-fat cheese with lettuce and tomato on light rye bread; delicious apple.
Friday	Chicken salad in pita bread with sliced green peppers; celery sticks; fresh pineapple chunks.

Week 2 — Lunches

Monday	Thinly sliced extra-lean ham and Mozzarella cheese with lettuce and tomato on thick crust French bread; raspberries.
Tuesday	Tuna with lettuce, tomato, onion and sprouts on dark rye bread; orange.
Wednesday	Sliced chicken with tomato and sprouts on sourdough bread; berries.
Thursday	Natural peanut butter on whole grain bread; celery and carrot sticks; sliced green pepper; banana.
Friday	Turkey with tomato, lettuce, sprouts and sliced mushrooms on whole wheat bread; pear.

These low-fat lunches actually provided more variety than did my pre-surgery meals. I soon enjoyed the new lunches more than the old. After about four months, I felt secure in my practice of the Positive Diet at lunch, and I decided to reward myself with a salami sandwich. As I walked into the deli, I was overwhelmed by the heady aroma of luncheon meats. I could almost taste how delicious the sandwich would be.

What a disappointment!

It was not delicious at all. The salami tasted greasy; it did not even look appealing. The sandwich had not changed. It was made the same as always. But I had changed, or, more specifically, my taste buds had changed. The Positive Diet had oriented them away from fatty foods. It was then that I knew that my lunch diet pattern had changed fundamentally and permanently. By following a few simple rules, I could keep my lunches under control. These rules were as follows:

▶ At the start of the diet, avoid all restaurant food, especially fast food.
▶ Reduce red meat lunches to no more than one per week; use poultry, fish and low-fat cheese instead.
▶ Avoid fatty luncheon meats such as bologna and frankfurters. Check the fat content of the so-called ''low-fat'' luncheon meats as many of these products are over 50% fat.
▶ Use safflower or corn oil mayonnaise and soft tub-style margarine as sandwich spreads.
▶ Use different breads and rolls for maximum sandwich variety.
▶ Take advantage of seasonal fresh fruits and vegetables.

84

Breakfast. On my old diet, breakfast had been a meal of extremes. On weekends I might eat a logger's meal of hash browns, bacon and eggs. On weekdays, I would eat no breakfast at all or I might have a cup of coffee and a roll. I decided to treat each type of breakfast separately.

Weekday breakfasts needed changing for two reasons. The first was to reduce whatever fat and cholesterol existed in the meal. This was done by using soft margarine on toast and by excluding commercially baked goods such as doughnuts, Danish pastry and sugar-coated buns. The second reason was to introduce additional healthful foods into my diet.

For example, research by Dr. James Anderson at the University of Kentucky has shown that oat bran, available as a hot breakfast cereal, can lower blood cholesterol. For that reason, I began to eat oat bran on a regular basis for breakfast. In addition, no breakfast or a poor breakfast could make me so ravenous by lunchtime that a Positive Diet lunch might not be sufficient. This could open opportunities for pastry at a coffee break or a bag of potato chips at lunch. However, if the breakfast fare could keep me satisfied until lunch, not only would I benefit nutritionally, but the chances for lunch success would be enhanced.

My new weekday breakfasts were planned around low-fat protein, whole grains and fresh fruits. The protein was in the form of natural peanut butter, low-fat cheeses, egg substitute, non-fat yogurt and skim milk; the whole grains were in the form of cereals, particularly oat bran, toast, bagels, muffins or bran muffins and the fruits were eaten in their natural state or squeezed into juice. A typical weekday meal plan would be as follows:

Week 1 — Breakfasts

Monday	$\frac{1}{2}$ grapefruit; Mozzarella cheese and fresh tomato slices broiled on a whole grain muffin.
Tuesday	Low-fat yogurt with fresh raspberries; crumpet with a dab of honey; skim milk.
Wednesday	Sliced banana; toasted bagel with natural peanut butter; skim milk.
Thursday	Chilled fresh melon; hot oatmeal or oat bran cereal; skim milk.
Friday	Fresh strawberries; scrambled eggs (egg substitute) with salsa; bran muffin.

Week 2 — Breakfasts

Monday	Freshly squeezed grapefruit juice; hot or cold cereal with skim milk; bran wheat toast.
Tuesday	Freshly squeezed orange juice; homemade oat bran muffin; skim milk.
Wednesday	Chilled orange slices; low-fat frozen yogurt; toasted muffin; skim milk.
Thursday	Baked apple; hot oatmeal or oat bran cereal with skim milk; whole wheat toast.
Friday	Chilled grapefruit; French toast made with crusty French bread; skim milk.

These breakfasts met my needs extremely well because:

>They did not take great forethought in planning.

>They did not take a great deal of time either to prepare or to eat.

>They offered sufficient variety.

>They were low in fat and in cholesterol.

>They kept me satisfied for the entire morning.

Weekend breakfasts were a different matter. On my old diet these frequently had been brunches, often including fresh fruit, sausage, ham, bacon, eggs, hash browns, pancakes, waffles or French toast. The fat and cholesterol in these meals were astronomical. The meats were fat, the eggs were high in cholesterol and almost everything except the fruit was fried in animal fat. I had two choices: I could either eliminate these breakfasts altogether or I could modify their content.

The first element to be examined was eggs. A single large chicken egg contains 251 mg. of cholesterol. The white of the egg contains 60% of the protein and only 1% of the cholesterol, while the yolk contains 40% of the protein and 99% of the cholesterol. For this reason, egg whites did not have to be removed from my diet, but only egg yolks.

Consequently, egg substitute (made from egg whites and unsaturated oil) was very important to the preservation of my weekend breakfasts. Egg substitute, available in the supermarket or made at home, allows breakfasts to include such foods as scrambled eggs, omelets, huevos rancheros, pancakes, French toast, waffles and crepes. By using egg substitute rather than whole eggs in these dishes, cholesterol was either reduced or eliminated, yet the taste and the appearance remained virtually unchanged. To further reduce cholesterol, these dishes were cooked on a non-stick teflon griddle or in a non-stick teflon frying pan, thus eliminating the need for fat or oil as a lubricant.

My last move was to eliminate breakfast meats. Pork sausage is 87% fat, bacon 82% fat, and ham 69% fat. These meats are also rich in cholesterol. One ounce (one link) of pork sausage contains 30 milligrams and 4 ounces of ham contains over 100 milligrams. It was only prudent to eliminate these foods from my diet.

REDUCING BUTTERFAT

The second basic principle, the reduction of butterfat, is concerned with the fat in whole milk and whole milk foods, such as cheese, cream and ice cream. Because butterfat is a saturated fat, it has the same negative impact upon the health of the heart and the blood vessels as does the saturated fat in red meat. Initially, it was difficult to relate dairy products to harmful saturated fat. These foods meant calcium and protein to me, essential elements for good health.

Food	% of Calories from Fat
Butter	99%
Double Cream	96%
Single Cream	88%
Sour Cream	88%
Cream Cheese	84%
Roquefort Cheese	74%
Cheddar Cheese	74%
Blue Cheese	73%
Parmesan Cheese	60%
Ice Cream	55%
Whole Milk	51%
Creamed Cottage Cheese	34%
Skimmed Milk	34%

Whole milk products are an important source of calcium and protein. But many also contain over 50% fat and are high in cholesterol as well. About one-third (100 mg.) of the recommended maximum daily cholesterol allowance can be reached by consuming any one of the following:
>3 cups of whole milk
>4 tablespoons of butter
>4 ounces of Cheddar cheese
>3 ounces of cream cheese
>⅔ cup of sour cream
>1 cup of ice cream

Once whole milk products were placed in their proper perspective, there was no alternative but to reduce their use.

Step Number 1: Identification of Butterfat Sources

Whole milk foods were consumed at virtually every meal on my old diet — whole or semi-skimmed breakfast, lunch and dinner; cheese in sandwiches and in casseroles; butter on bread and in cooking; cream in cheese, snacks, and desserts; and ice cream in cones, milkshakes and floats.

Step Number 2: Reduction of Butterfat

I began by applying the second basic principle to whole milk. My first move was to eliminate it in favor of semi-skimmed milk. Touted as "low-fat" by the dairy industry, I assumed that this milk contained very little fat. As such, it would be extremely low in saturated fat. Unfortunately this is not the case. This milk may be lower in fat than whole milk, but it is not a "low-fat" product. As far as the heart and blood vessels are concerned semi-skimmed milk is "high-fat."

The only genuine low-fat alternative is skim

milk. Virtually none of its calories are derived from butterfat, yet it has all the benefits of whole milk (calcium, protein) and none of the drawbacks (high butterfat). In addition, skim milk had a much lower cholesterol value than whole milk.

It took about a month to get used to the taste of skim milk. Initially, I found that adding ⅓ cup of powdered milk to each quart of skim milk produced a creamier taste. After a while, I began to prefer the lighter taste of skim milk to the creamier taste of semi-skimmed or whole milk, and I no longer needed to add the milk powder.

There was another benefit to the change: my total milk consumption decreased. At first I did not care for the taste of skim milk; and by the time I came to like it, I was already used to drinking less milk.

Butter was another source of fat. I used it on toast, pancakes, waffles or French toast; on rolls, bread or in sandwiches; on potatoes, rice or vegetables; and in snacks, such as pies, cakes, cookies or popcorn. Not only is butter over 80% fat, but over half of its fat content is saturated. In addition, butter is high in cholesterol.

I eliminated butter in favor of soft tub-style margarine. I always made sure that the prime ingredient was liquid safflower oil or corn oil and the amount of unsaturated fat was at least double the amount of saturated fat. Once again label reading was very important. Tub-style margarine does not need to hold its shape and is less hydrogenated than is stick margarine, which contains saturated fat because of the hardening process.

The change to soft tub-style margarine minimized the amount of saturated fat consumed. The change did not, however, reduce the total amount of fat consumed. In order to do that, I followed these steps:

▶Reduce by ½ the amount of margarine used on rolls, toast, pancakes . . . After a time, reduce this amount again by ¼.

▶Avoid commercially baked goods, such as rolls, pastries, pies, cakes and doughnuts.

▶Avoid the use of buttersauce on potatoes, rice, vegetables and main dishes; instead use herbs, spices, flavored vinegar or lemon juice. Dip shellfish, such as crab, clams, mussels and lobster in fresh lemon juice, rather than butter. Avoid foods fried or sautéed in butter or margarine. For home cooking use a non-stick teflon pan or use lemon juice, flavored vinegar, vermouth, wine, broth or water.

▶Beware of restaurant foods. Generally, they are rich in butter and/or margarine. Ask how the food is prepared. If it's fried in butter, do not order it. Do not assume anything — ask questions! A broiled or barbecued salmon fillet may automatically be served with a butter sauce.

Cheese was another dairy food that called for modification. Most cheese is rich in cholesterol. As much as I loved cheeseburgers, and Swiss or Cheddar cheese on sandwiches, it was only prudent to remove this fat source from my diet. I did this by substituting non-fat and low-fat cheese for that made with cream and whole milk.

Many types of low-fat cheese are available. Cottage cheese is quite low-fat and is suitable as a spread on crackers and vegetables and as a dip. Hoop cheese and part-skim-milk Mozzarella can be sliced and are suitable for sandwiches. Other types of low-fat cheese include Ricotta, Edam, Somerset, Danbo and Cheddar. Remember, however, that all low-fat cheese is still relatively high in fat and should be eaten judiciously.

Since much of this cheese is produced in a high-fat as well as a low-fat variety, label reading becomes very important. The low-fat varieties are generally made from skim or partially skim milk.

Some cheese may be labeled "low-fat", but the fat content may still be over 50%.

In my opinion, a true low-fat cheese should have a fat content of 20% or less.

A trip to a speciality cheese store can be very rewarding if the salesperson is knowledgable. These stores usually carry the newest varieties of low-fat cheese and the salespeople generally know the fat content of each cheese as well.

Other dairy products, such as cottage cheese and yogurt, are available in low-fat versions. However, the fat content often is considered low only when contrasted with that of its whole milk counterpart.

Sweet cream, ice cream and whipped cream made from whole milk are too rich in saturated fat to be acceptable on a heart-healthy diet. But with creative substitution, homemade recipes for these foods exist, allowing low-fat variations to be periodically enjoyed (see pages 114 and 295–6).

SUMMING UP FAT AND CHOLESTEROL

The Positive Diet is not totally free of foods that contain fat, butterfat and cholesterol. However, these elements can be drastically reduced using a few simple guidelines:

▶Make use of meal planning and creative substitution.
▶Avoid high-cholesterol foods such as liver, kidneys and other organ meats.
▶Reduce whole egg consumption; use egg substitute or egg whites.
▶Avoid red meats rich in saturated fat such as sausage, bacon and luncheon meats; use more poultry and fish.
▶When red meat is eaten, reduce the portion size; use a lean grade trimmed of all visible fat; broil,

roast, bake or barbecue, but never fry; cook to medium or well-done.
► De-fat meat drippings and broths before using.
► Always cook poultry without the skin; choose white meat over dark.
► Sauté in wine, broth, water, vermouth or flavored vinegar or use a non-stick pan; never sauté in hydrogenated margarine, lard, butter or shortening.
► Oils of choice include olive, safflower and corn. Avoid butter and stick margarine; instead, use soft tub-type margarine made from liquid vegetable oil; reduce the amount of margarine used.
► Avoid whole milk and whole milk products; use skim milk and low-fat cheese.
► Learn to read labels.
► Avoid convenience foods and commercially baked goods; beware of restaurant food, especially fast food.
► Increase complex carbohydrates (vegetables, fruit, grains and legumes).

REDUCING SALT

The third basic principle of the Positive Diet addresses the reduction of salt and sodium. I had eaten salt-rich foods, such as pickles, bacon, and potato chips. I used salt in cooking and at the table and I used processed foods, such as soups, pork and beans, chili and frozen hash brown potatoes. It was time to re-educate my taste buds.

Step Number 1: Identifying Salt Sources

The sources of salt on my pre-surgery diet could be divided into two categories: obvious and hidden. Obvious sources are those in which salt is expected to be found, such as potato chips or pickles. Hidden sources are those in which salt is a surprise ingredient, such as certain brands of peanut butter or dehydrated chicken noodle or onion soup.

The obvious sources included:
>table salt used as a condiment
>table salt used in cooking as a seasoning
>table salt used in alcoholic drinks, such as in Bloody Marys
>salty condiments, such as seasoning salt, soy sauce and bouillon cubes
>salty foods, such as pickles, olives, anchovies, salted herring, sauerkraut, potato chips, pretzels, popcorn and salted nuts.

The hidden sources included:
>processed luncheon meats, such as bologna, salami, and frankfurters
>ham, bacon, sausage and cured pork
>canned tuna or salmon packed in oil
>cheese and cheese spreads
>vegetable juice and tomato juice
>canned tomato sauce, paste and pureé
>commercial salad dressings
>condiments such as ketchup, relish, chili sauce and mustard
>fast food hamburgers, French fries, chicken, tacos and pizza
>commercially baked bread, crackers, rolls, breadsticks, pastry and desserts
>cereals and pancake mixes
>salted butter and margarine
>bicarbonate of soda and powder
>canned, frozen and dehydrated processed foods such as chili, macaroni and cheese, TV dinners, and canned vegetables

Step Number 2: Salt Reduction

The Obvious Sources. I used table salt regularly on my old diet. I salted all food even before it was tasted. This was an automatic, knee-jerk reaction. In order to curtail salting, I had to remove the salt from the table. So I threw the salt shaker away!

In the beginning this proved to be a problem. Saltless food tasted bland and I longed to spice up meals with a dash of salt. I resisted this temptation by reminding myself of the importance of salt reduction to cardiac health and by handling the reduction one day at a time. "Certainly you can last one day without your salt shaker," I told myself each morning.

Soon a month had elapsed and I noticed a subtle change taking place in my taste buds. I began to enjoy the natural flavor of the saltless foods. A tossed green salad with fresh vegetables, for example, contained a myriad of pleasing tastes. In the past it had existed merely as a vehicle for carrying salt. Now, with my taste buds no longer dulled, I could taste the many distinct flavors. I also began to appreciate other sources of seasonings — black pepper, garlic powder, parsley, tarragon, chili powder and lemon juice. Meals could be spiced up I learned, without using my salt shaker.

After about two months of eating in this manner, I decided to test my taste buds. I made a large salad and salted it just as I had on my old diet. The taste of the salad was not like I had remembered. It was too salty to be enjoyable; there was no taste to the food itself. I might as well have been eating cardboard. It was then that I knew that my desire for salt could be diminished permanently and that I could live and eat well without my salt shaker.

The next step was to reduce the amount of salt used in cooking by 25%. If a recipe called for 1 teaspoon of salt, I used only ¾ teaspoon. Much to my delight, I found there was very little change in the taste of the food. After a few months, I made a second reduction of 25%, again without adverse results. And finally, I made a third reduction of 25%. I further reduced the amount of salt when cooking with processed foods such as canned tomatoes, tomato sauce, tomato paste or chicken broth, as these foods are already high in sodium. To bring out the natural flavors of foods, I relied on lemon juice, flavored vinegars and herbs and spices which were low in sodium. Black pepper or sage, for example, each contain less than 1 milligram of sodium per teaspoon; the same amount of salt contains 2300 milligrams of sodium.

Finally, I restricted or eliminated those foods which were obviously too salty to be on a heart-healthy diet. Such foods were easy to identify, for to taste them was to know they were rich in salt. Keeping in mind that an "adequate and safe" sodium level is no more than 3300 milligrams daily, it was easy to see how such foods could cause that level to be exceeded.

In some instances low- or no-salt versions were available, such as unsalted peanuts or potato chips. But for foods such as pickles, sauerkraut or salted herring, where no viable substitute existed, drastic reduction or total elimination was the only answer.

The Hidden Sources. With the obvious sources of salt under control, I turned my attention to the more difficult problem of controlling the hidden sources. The solution lay in totally revising my dependance upon processed foods.

In researching hidden salt, I was shocked at the number of canned, frozen and dehydrated foods in which salt and other sodium products are main ingredients. The same was true for fast foods.

The amount of salt and sodium included in processed foods is incredible, especially when contrasted with the sodium content of these same foods in their natural state. Peas, for example, contain just .9 milligrams of sodium per serving; the same amount of canned peas contains 230 mg. An ear of corn contains about 1 mg. of sodium, a cup of canned corn about 384 mg. Three ounces of steak contain 55 mg., a frozen meat loaf dinner about 1304 mg. Three ounces of pork contain 59 mg., the same amount of canned ham about 1114 mg. Processed foods, a mainstay of the heat and serve Western diet pattern, guarantee that our sodium intake is high enough to be a health hazard.

Not all processed foods contain the same level of sodium. Food processors face relatively few restrictions in the use of salt or other sodium additives such as sodium benzoate, sodium nitrate, monosodium glutamate, sodium bicarbonate or sodium phosphate, as far as their use as food additives is concerned and that is the way most food processors want it.

With no requirement existing for food proc- essors to display specific sodium information, even the most prudent shopper is at a disadvantage when purchasing processed foods. This situation may change in the future as more and more organizations demand such information.

Under the present circumstances, consumers can take only one step to protect themselves. Adopt a simple rule not to purchase any processed food that lists salt or sodium as one of the first three ingredients on the label. While this rule provides less than a precise measurement, it does provide an acceptable standard against which processed foods can be measured.

The only true solution to the high-salt problem is to incorporate more natural foods into the diet. These foods are fresher, taste better, and are significantly lower in salt, sodium and other additives than are processed foods. They are the key to a successful low-sodium diet.

SUMMING UP SALT

The Positive Diet is not salt-free. However, it is designed to restrict excessive salt and sodium consumption through the use of a few guidelines:
▶ Avoid using salt as a condiment; remove the salt shaker from the table.
▶ Reduce the salt called for in recipes by 25% initially, by 75% ultimately; never add salt to processed foods.
▶ Avoid using sodium-rich seasonings, seasoning salt, and soy sauce; use low-sodium alternatives such as garlic, onion, lemon juice, flavored vinegars, fresh herbs and spices.
▶ Avoid obviously salty foods such as pickles, salted nuts, salted potato chips and sauerkraut.
▶ Avoid fast foods; they specialize in high-salt.
▶ Avoid processed foods as much as possible. When using them, read food labels carefully. If sodium content is high (one of the first three ingredients), avoid the food. For best results, consult a sodium dictionary.
▶ Use more natural foods. Take advantage of fresh raw fruits, berries and vegetables in season.

REDUCING SUGAR

The fourth basic principle of the Positive Diet calls for a reduction of sugar. I had not considered my old diet to be rich in sugar, but a close examination revealed multiple sources. Refined sugar was

used in cooking and baking, sometimes as a condiment on fruits or berries, and as an ingredient
in ice cream, soft drinks, cookies, canned fruit,
and even processed spaghetti sauce and canned
soup.

Step Number 1: Identification of Concentrated
Sugar Sources

As with salt, the sugar sources could be classified
as obvious and hidden. The obvious sources constituted about 36% of the concentrated sugar intake; and the hidden sources about 64%.
    The obvious sources included:
>granulated sugar, powdered sugar, and brown
  sugar used on cereal, fruit, berries, and in coffee
>granulated sugar, powdered sugar and brown
  sugar used as an ingredient in cooking and
  baking
>granulated sugar used in drinks, such as iced
  tea and lemonade.
    The hidden sources include the following:
>candy and sugary snacks, such as gum drops,
  mints, and chocolate bars
>soft drinks, such as soda pop and cocoa mixes
>ice cream, milk shakes, flavored milk
>commercially baked pastry and desserts, such
  as doughnuts, pies, cakes, cupcakes; frostings
>commercially baked bread, crackers, rolls, bis-
  cuits and breadsticks
>jams, jellies, marmalades
>sugared breakfast cereals
>canned fruits
>cured meats
>salad dressings, ketchup and other such condi-
  ments.
>peanut butter
>processed convenience foods such as baked
  beans, tomato sauce, soups

Step Number 2: Sugar Reduction

The Obvious Sources centered around refined table
sugar. My first action was to remove the sugar
bowl from the table. Initially, the sugarless food
often tasted bland. Again, the one-day-at-a-time
method was employed. By never looking forward
more than 24 hours, the reduction of sugar became
a short-term problem. Within six weeks, my taste
buds became acclimatized to the natural taste of
foods. I began to relish new flavors and textures.
A bowl of blueberries could now be appreciated
for its natural sweetness; to add sugar was to gild
the lily. The natural flavor of fruit, cereal and other
foods more than compensated for the loss of the
super-sweet table sugar.

The second area where concentrated sugar
posed a problem was with baked goods and
candy. A 4-ounce piece of iced chocolate cake
contains 10 teaspoons of sugar; a 1-ounce square
of fudge contains 4½ teaspoons. There was no
way to reconcile this amount of concentrated
sugar with a healthy diet pattern.

Fortunately, by the time I began to work on the
sugar problem, a break away from many of these
foods had already been made due to their high fat
content. In their place I substituted fresh fruit. A
ripe peach became as satisfying to my sweet tooth
as a milkshake or a candy bar. I also used nuts and
sunflower seeds to replace sugary snacks. As my
need for sugar gradually decreased, so did my
desire.

There were certain occasions when cakes or
pies were appropriate, such as a birthday or
Thanksgiving. For these special times, I used
low-fat ingredients and reduced the sugar and the
salt as much as possible. It is important to keep
these special occasions to a minimum so as not to

negatively impact cardiac health.

The most difficult area to control was the hidden sugar used as an additive in processed foods and beverages. Sugar is often a surprise ingredient in such foods as frozen chicken dinners, baked beans and non-dairy creamers. It can even be found as an ingredient in certain pipe tobacco!

Many food processors routinely add concentrated sugar during processing for sweetening, moisture control, and spoilage control. For that reason, label reading is essential. Food processors are required to list on the label all ingredients in the food product in decreasing order according to weight. Only by identifying the position of sugar on the ingredient list can the sugar content of the food be approximated.

Even with careful label reading, however, the consumer must be very aware. In a study conducted by Washington State University and the U.S. Department of Agriculture, a cereal recently test-marketed by one food manufacturer was shown to contain granulated table sugar, brown sugar and corn syrup. Also contained as ingredients were four cereal grains — refined white flour, corn flour, degermed corn meal and rice flour. The food manufacturer circumvented the listing of sugar as the main ingredient by grouping the four flours into a single "cereal grain" category and by listing the three sugars separately, thus giving the impression that the cereal was made up chiefly of grain. The label did not change the fact that concentrated sugar was the primary ingredient in the cereal; it only served to confuse the consumer about the real sugar content of the product.

Label reading is further complicated because concentrated sugar can be identified under various names: sugar, sucrose, glucose, maltose, dextrose, lactose, fructose, malt, corn solids, corn syrup, honey, molasses and invert sugar. A good rule is to avoid the food if any of these items are among the first three on the list of ingredients.

Two other areas of concern were alcoholic beverages and soft drinks. Alcohol is a concentrated sugar and one which can quickly saturate the sugar storing capacity of the body while providing little nutritional value. And soft drinks contain non-nutritive carbonated water, colorings, flavorings, and in the case of colas, caffeine. In addition, they are about 9% concentrated sugar. One can contains 5-9 teaspoons.

There is no short cut to achieving a low-sugar diet. Where processed foods and beverages, snack foods, candy and alcohol constitute much of the diet, high sugar intake is assured. It is only through the elimination of these sugar sources and the institution of fresh foods in their place that a permanent reduction in concentrated sugar intake can take place.

SUMMING UP SUGAR

The Positive Diet is not totally free of concentrated sugar. However, it is designed to restrict excessive sugar consumption through the use of a few simple rules:

▶Remove refined sugar from the table; avoid using concentrated sugar as a sweetener.
▶Reduce concentrated sugar called for in homemade recipes by ⅓.
▶Avoid sugary foods, such as candy, soft drinks, ice cream, cake.
▶Use more fresh fruit.
▶Drink alcohol only in moderation.

▶Read food labels carefully. If concentrated sugar is listed as one of the first three ingredients, avoid the food. Know all the names for concentrated sugar.

WEIGHT CONTROL TIPS

There are certain actions which can be taken to enhance the opportunity for weight control on the Positive Diet.

▶Make a commitment to staying on the Positive Diet. Too often a healthy, weight reducing approach to eating is defeated not by the stomach but by the head.

▶Use meal planning for all regular meals. This will enable you to plan to avoid foods which are high in calories.

▶Eat balanced meals. Be sure to include fresh fruits and vegetables at every meal; they are low in calories and high in bulk and will keep you satisfied between meals.

▶Avoid second helpings. If you must have seconds, they should be of vegetables and fruits rather than of the entreé.

▶Watch out for hunger between meals. Often times it is a false hunger brought on by nervousness about the dietary change. Combat it with fresh raw vegetables. Keep a bowl of cut up vegetables on ice in the refrigerator for snacks. When hunger or nervousness moves you to eat between meals, vegetables can keep your jaws occupied.

▶Ban calorically dense foods from the house. Why tempt yourself with cookies, cakes and candy? For desserts, use fresh fruit.

▶Moderate the use of alcohol. Instead of pre-dinner cocktails and hors d'oeuvres, drink mineral water and munch on raw vegetables with low-fat cottage cheese or tomato salsa. This provides the relaxation and satisfaction of the cocktail hour at only a fraction of the calories.

▶If you are counting calories closely, use a food scale to weigh your food. This will give you exact portions and maximum calorie control.

▶Beware of restaurant food, especially at the beginning of the diet. A single high-calorie meal can undo a week or more of successful weight reducing efforts.

COOKBOOK

CHAPTER SIX

MEAL PLANNING

GUIDE TO BASIC FOODS

Recommended	Not Recommended
chicken	duck
turkey	goose
fish	spareribs
most shellfish	mutton
rabbit	sausage
venison	bacon
beef*	frankfurters
lamb*	luncheon meats
pork*	heavily marbled meats
ham*	fatty meats
	shrimp
lima beans	smoked salmon
lentils	kidney
chick peas	liver
split peas	heart
	sweetbreads
egg whites	
egg substitute	egg yolks
	(limit to 3 per week)
fortified skim milk	
fortified skim milk powder	whole milk
evaporated milk	semi-skimmed milk
low-fat yogurt	egg nog
low-fat ice cream	chocolate whole milk
	whole milk yogurt
	low-fat yogurt
	whole milk buttermilk
	ice cream
	cream
	sour cream
	whipped cream
	non-dairy cream substitute

*occasional use only

Recommended	Not Recommended
some to look for *include:*	cream cheese
	cheese spreads
	creamed cottage cheese
Cottage cheese	whole milk cheese or
Quark	cheese made with cream
Sapsago	*some to look for*
Dry Cottage Cheese	*include:*
Danbo	
Mozzarella	Swiss
low-fat Cheddar	Brie
	Camembert
most vegetables	whole milk Cheddar
	Roquefort
	Blue Cheese
	olives
	avocados
most fresh fruits	pickles
	sauerkraut
	all brined vegetables
safflower oil	all pickled vegetables
soybean oil	
sunflower oil	fruits canned in heavy
corn oil	syrup
cottonseed oil	
sesame oil	coconut oil
olive oil	palm oil
peanut oil	hydrogenated vegetable
tub-style safflower oil	shortening
margarine	lard
safflower oil mayonnaise	suet
	chicken fat
	pork fat
	meat fat
	cube margarine
	butter

108

Recommended	Not Recommended
traditional style peanut butter	highly processed peanut butter
cocoa powder*	coconut
	milk chocolate
	baking chocolate
bagels	sweet rolls
Muffins	biscuits
French bread	doughnuts
pumpernickel	cheese bread
rye bread	egg bread
whole wheat bread	flour tortillas
pita bread	(made with lard)
Wholemeal and rye crispbreads	most crackers
whole grain cereals	
brown rice	sugared cereals
barley	coconut cereals
bulgar	prepared rice mixes
durum pasta	
most un-salted peanuts	egg noodles
	packaged cake mixes
	commercially baked goods
	most potato and corn chips
	Macadamia nuts
	cashews

* occasional use only

TABLE OF SUBSTITUTIONS

Rather Than	Substitute
Whole Egg	Beat together 1 egg white, 2 teaspoons milk powder, and 2 teaspoons safflower oil *or use* 2 egg whites *or use* commercially prepared egg substitute.
Whole Milk (1 cup)	Fortify 1 cup skim milk with 1 cup milk powder *or combine* 1 cup skim milk plus 2 tablespoons safflower oil.
Buttermilk (1 cup)	Heat 1 cup skim milk to room temperature; add 1 tablespoon lemon juice. Let stand 5 minutes; beat *or make* homemade using a cultured food processor.
Whipped Cream	Combine $\frac{1}{3}$ cup ice water, 1 tablespoon lemon juice, $\frac{3}{4}$ teaspoon vanilla essence, $\frac{1}{3}$ cup milk powder, beat 10 minutes or until stiff; add 2 tablespoons sugar.
Whole Milk Yogurt	Prepare homemade low-fat yogurt using an inexpensive yogurt maker or cultured food processor.
Sour Cream	Plain low-fat yogurt *or prepare* low-fat sour cream

Ice Cream	Prepare low-fat using an ice cream freezer.
Whole Milk Cheese	Low-fat cheese — ask your dairyman to verify percentage of fat.
Parmesan Cheese Romano Cheese	Sapsago Cheese, grated *or for a milder flavor* Mozzarella or Danbo.
Butter Margarine Shortening	Use tub style safflower margarine *or use* safflower oil.

Proportion	*Proportion safflower oil*
1 tablespoon	1 tablespoon
2 tablespoons	1½ tablespoons
⅓ cup	4 tablespoons
½ cup	6 tablespoons
¾ cup	9 tablespoons

Highly processed Peanut Butter	Old-fashioned style peanut butter
Mayonnaise	Homemade safflower mayonnaise *or* Commercially made safflower mayonnaise
Cream Soup	Homemade cream soup *or* thicken homemade chicken or beef broth with flour, arrowroot or grated raw potato.
Chicken Broth Beef Broth	Homemade de-fatted, low sodium broth

Bouillon Cube (1 cube)	1 cup homemade chicken or beef broth — reduce liquid in recipe requiring bouillon cube to compensate.
Baking Chocolate Baking Chocolate (1 oz. square)	3 tablespoons cocoa powder plus 1 tablespoon safflower oil

SKIM MILK

1½   cups milk powder
3¾   cups water

Combine milk powder and water in a covered container; shake vigorously.

Note: Always buy milk powder that is fortified with vitamins A and D.
For a creamier flavor increase milk powder by ⅓ cup.

EGG SUBSTITUTE

1   egg white
2¼   teaspoons milk powder
2   teaspoons safflower oil

Combine ingredients in a blender; whirl.
Yield is the equivalent of 1 egg.

Note: Egg substitute keeps 1 week in the refrigerator and may be frozen. Recipe may be multiplied.

WHIPPED CREAM SUBSTITUTE

⅓ cup ice water
1¼ teaspoons lemon juice
½ teaspoon vanilla essence
⅓ cup milk powder
2 tablespoons sugar

Combine water, lemon juice and vanilla; stir in milk powder, Beat 5–10 minutes or until stiff; add sugar. Beat 1–2 minutes.

Note: If topping should separate, beat again just before serving.

PLAIN LOW-FAT YOGURT

1 quart skim milk
⅓ cup milk powder
1 heaped tablespoon plain low-fat
    yogurt

Combine skim milk and dry milk powder in a 2-quart saucepan; heat just to boiling. Remove from heat; cool. Measure milk temperature with the thermometer that accompanies the yogurt maker; when mercury reaches the "add starter" level on the thermometer, stir in 1 tablespoon low-fat yogurt. Process according to manufacturer's instructions. Refrigerate several hours before serving.

Note: Yogurt will keep several weeks in the refrigerator. Be sure to save some to use as starter for the next batch.

FRUIT YOGURT

1 recipe plain low-fat yogurt* (page 114)
  fresh or frozen fruits or
    berries, puréed in the blender

Method 1: Fill the bottom of each yogurt cup with ⅓ cup of puréed fruit, such as strawberries, raspberries, blackberries or blueberries. Prepare low-fat yogurt as directed in preceeding recipe; pour over puréed fruits. Process as directed.

Method 2: Prepare low-fat yogurt; process as directed. Chill. Just before serving add ⅓ cup of chilled puréed fruit to each cup of yogurt. Stir.

HERB SEASONING

1 tablespoon garlic powder
½ teaspoon cayenne pepper
1 teaspoon ground basil
1 teaspoon ground marjoram
1 teaspoon ground thyme
1 teaspoon ground parsley
1 teaspoon ground savory
1 teaspoon ground mace
1 teaspoon onion powder
1 teaspoon black pepper
1 teaspoon ground sage

Combine seasonings; pour into a salt shaker. Use in place of salt.
Reproduced with permission by the American Heart Association.

When planning menus strive for balanced meals. Include a protein portion, such as fish, poultry, red meat, peanut butter, cheese, legumes, egg, or egg substitute; a grain portion, such as potatoes, rice, pasta, bread or cereal; a vegetable portion; and a fruit portion.

Whenever possible choose fresh vegetables and fresh fruits. For best value, select from those which are in season.

UK PUBLISHER'S NOTES ON THE RECIPES

This book was originally published in the United States and, consequently, some terminology and ingredients may be unfamiliar to British and Commonwealth readers. To overcome any problems this may cause, a glossary of terms and ingredients has been compiled, which can be found on pages 118–119.

OVEN TEMPERATURES

Fahrenheit	Centigrade	Gas Mark	Heat Level
225	110	¼	very cool
250	130	½	very cool
275	140	1	cool or slow
300	150	2	cool or slow
325	170	3	warm
350	180	4	moderate
375	190	5	moderately hot
400	200	6	fairly hot
425	220	7	hot
450	230	8	very hot
475	240	9	very hot

TABLE OF METRIC EQUIVALENTS

Here are some standard measurements that every cook will find useful.

Measurements by volume
   1 teaspoon = ⅓ tablespoon = 5 milliliters
   1½ teaspoons = ½ tablespoon
   3 teaspoons = 1 tablespoon = 15 milliliters
   4 tablespoons = ¼ cup = 59 milliliters
   5⅓ tablespoons = ⅓ cup = 79 milliliters
   8 tablespoons = ½ cup = 79 milliliters
   16 tablespoons = 1 cup
   1 cup = 8 fluid ounces = .2366 liters (approx. ¼ liter)
   2 cups = 1 pint = .4732 liters (approx. ½ liter)
   4 cups or 2 pints = 1 quart = .9463 liters (approx. 1 liter)
   4 quarts = 1 gallon

Measurements by weight
   1 ounce = approx. 28 grams
   3½ ounces = 100 grams
   16 ounces = 1 pound
   1 pound = 454 grams
   2.2 pounds = 1 kilogram
All measurements refer to the level amount unless otherwise specified.

1 U.S. pint = 16 fl oz (1 Imperial pint = 20 fl oz)
1 U.S. quart = 32 fl oz
1 U.S. cup = 8 fl oz (1 Imperial cup = 10 fl oz)
To measure an American cupful, fill to 8 fl oz on a measuring jug.

117

GLOSSARY

all-purpose flour — plain flour
garbanzo beans — chick peas
baking soda — bicarbonate of soda
baking pan — baking tin
baking shells — pastry cases
bibb lettuce — soft leaf lettuce
broil (verb) — toast, grill
bulgar wheat — parboiled cracked wheat
cake pan — cake tin
Cantaloupe — small, scented melon
club soda — soda water
celery root — celeriac
cheese:
  Farmer cheese — use low-fat cottage cheese
  Jack — mild, melting cheese, use Cheddar or Cheshire
  pot cheese — use low-fat cottage cheese
  Ricotta — soft, bland, white, uncured, low-fat Italian cheese
  cookie — biscuit
  cornstarch — cornflour
  eggplant — aubergine
  ground — minced
  extract — essence, for example, vanilla essence
  flowerets — florets
  griddle — omelette pan
  grinder — food mill
  ground round — mince
  Jalapeno pepper — hot chilli pepper, available in tins or jars
  loaf pan — loaf tin
  muffin cups — fairy cake tins
  minced — finely chopped
  non-hydrogenated peanut butter — traditional-type peanut butter,
    processed as little as possible
  pie pan — pie dish
  pitted — stones removed
  potato starch — potato flour

118

romaine — cos lettuce
skillet — frying pan
skim milk — skimmed milk
snow peas — mange-tout peas
Swiss chard — spinach beet
tacos — crisp, fried Mexican cornmeal pancakes
tomato paste — tomato purée
tomatoes:
  plum — small Italian cooking tomatoes
  Note: American tomatoes are generally bigger than British ones,
      you may need to increase numbers in recipes accordingly

tortillas — Mexican cornmeal pancakes
water-pack tunafish — not readily available, substitute tuna packed
  in vegetable oil, drain well and rinse before using
zucchini — courgettes

Don't Eat Your Heart Out

COOKING EQUIPMENT AND STAPLES

You need not buy a lot of sophisticated cooking equipment to implement the Positive Diet. A teflon skillet, teflon griddle, teflon baking sheets and teflon cake pans are essential. And an inexpensive yogurt maker is very useful, as is a vegetable steamer, wire whisk, blender and an electric mixer.

The following is a list of staples which are frequently used on the Positive Diet:

Milk Powder
Egg Substitute
Low-fat Cheese
Low-fat Yogurt*
Non-hydrogenated
    Peanut Butter
Water-Pack Tuna Fish
Lemon Juice
Fruit Juices
Fresh Fruits
Chicken Broth*
Beef Broth*
Canned Tomatoes*

Safflower Mayonnaise
Safflower Oil
Olive Oil
Tub Safflower Margarine
Dijon Mustard
Whole Grain Breads
Whole Grain Natural
    Cereals
Flour
Yeast
Fresh Vegetables
Tomato Puree**
Tomato Paste**
Tomato Sauce**

*Preferably Homemade
**Preferably Unsalted or Homemade

120

COOKING TERMS AND PROCEDURES

TO STORE FRESH GARLIC peel the cloves and place them in a jar; cover with safflower oil. Store covered in refrigerator.

GARLIC-SAFFLOWER OIL is the oil that covers the garlic — see preceding tip on storing fresh garlic.

GINGER JUICE is made by grating a piece of fresh ginger and then squeezing the pulp for the juice.

RECIPE PROPORTIONS: Most recipes in this book serve 4. The proportions are such that they may easily be cut in half and in most cases in half again, or they may easily be doubled.

IMPORTANT: Some recipe ingredients in the Positive Diet Book are followed by an asterisk (*). This indicates that for the recipe to be prepared in the most heart-healthy form, the particular ingredient involved should first be prepared according to instructions in this book. For example, if Chicken Broth* is listed as an ingredient, the asterisk means to use only homemade chicken broth (prepared from the recipe for Chicken Broth in this book).

The most common recipe ingredients followed by an asterisk are Chicken Broth and Low-Fat Yogurt. For this reason, it is convenient to keep some made up and on hand.

CHAPTER ELEVEN

APPETIZERS AND BEVERAGES

MARINATED SALMON

¾   cup fresh lime juice
¾   cup onion, finely chopped
1   stalk celery, finely chopped
2   tomatoes, peeled and chopped
¾   teaspoon or less salt
¾   teaspoon pepper
¾   teaspoon sugar
3-4   drops Tabasco sauce
1   pound fresh salmon, boned, skinned,
      and cut into 1-inch cubes
      fresh parsley for garnish
      fresh lemon wedges for garnish
      cherry tomatoes, halved, for garnish
1   white onion, sliced into rings for
      garnish

Combine lime juice, onion, celery, tomatoes, salt, pepper, sugar and Tabasco; pour over salmon. Toss; cover. Chill at least 6 hours; drain. To serve, cover a bed of fresh parsley with onion rings. Arrange salmon over top; ring with cherry tomatoes and lemon wedges.

Note: Serve as an hors d'oeuvre with French bread or for a light supper or for breakfast with bread and fresh fruit.

ARTICHOKES WITH FRESH LEMON

fresh artichokes
fresh lemon juice
safflower mayonnaise* (page 182)

Wash artichokes. Cut 1-inch off top. Cut off stem and tips of leaves. Place upside down in a deep dish.

To Pan-Steam: Place artichokes upright on steamer rack over boiling water. Pour ½ cup fresh lemon juice over artichokes. Cover pan tightly with lid. Steam 30-40 minutes or until tender.

To Microwave: Pour 4 tablespoons of lemon juice and 2 tablespoons of water over each artichoke. Cover dish with plastic wrap; prick a hole in the top of plastic wrap to allow steam to escape. For 1 medium artichoke allow 5-7 minutes cooking time; for 2 medium artichokes allow 7-9 minutes.

To Oven-Steam: Pour ½ cup of lemon juice over each artichoke. Cover dish with aluminum foil. Bake at 350° 30-40 minutes.

Artichokes are done when bottom leaves pull off easily; do not overcook.

Serve with homemade safflower mayonnaise.

Variation: Serve with Dijon vinaigrette* (page 183).

DIJON CUCUMBER STICKS

fresh cucumbers
Dijon vinaigrette* (page 183)

Peel cucumbers; cut lengthwise into eighths.
Serve with Dijon vinaigrette.

MARINATED MUSHROOMS

1	pound fresh mushrooms
	juice of 1 lemon
1	lemon, cut into thin rounds
¾	cup safflower oil
¼	cup cider vinegar
2	cloves garlic
¼	teaspoon pepper
1	teaspoon or less salt
	fresh parsley for garnish

Clean mushrooms; trim stems. Place in a large
saucepan; toss with lemon juice. Add oil, vinegar,
garlic, pepper and salt. Cook over medium-high
heat 20-30 minutes, stirring frequently. Remove
from heat; cool to room temperature. Chill. Drain.
Cover a serving plate with fresh parsley; top with
lemon rounds. Spoon mushrooms over lemons.

Note: Mushrooms will keep several days in the
refrigerator. Remaining marinade may be used
again for marinated mushrooms, as a marinade
for artichoke hearts or as a salad dressing.

SPRING ROLLS

2 dozen spring roll (lumpia) wrappers
2 tablespoons ginger juice* (page 121)
3 chicken breasts, diced
1 teaspoon sake
1 teaspoon salt-reduced soy sauce
¼ pound bamboo shoots, washed and
   cut into 2-inch strings
3-4 green onions, cut into thin strings
   2-inches in length
5-6 Shitake mushrooms, thinly sliced
½ cup fresh bean sprouts
½ teaspoon potato starch
½ cup water

Thaw spring roll wrappers. Grate ginger; squeeze juice from pulp over chicken. Sprinkle chicken with sake and soy sauce; let stand 20 minutes. Brown chicken in a teflon skillet over medium heat; set aside. Sauté bamboo shoots and onions in a small amount of water or chicken broth using a wok or heavy skillet; when barely tender, add mushrooms and bean sprouts; cook 2-3 minutes. Cool to room temperature.

In small saucepan, bring potato starch and water to a boil. Remove from heat; cool to room temperature.

Separate spring roll wrappers; lay them flat. Toss vegetables with chicken; place 3-4 table-spoons of mixture in the center of each wrapper. Brush outside edges of wrappers with mixture of potato starch and water; fold edges over envelope style. Seal outside seam with potato starch and water paste.

Brown spring rolls in a teflon skillet over medium heat 10 minutes or until very hot, or
Continued

brown in a heavy skillet using a very small amount of safflower oil — just enough to coat bottom of pan.

To reheat, warm in hot oven or in a microwave oven.

Note: Spring roll (lumpia) wrappers and Shitake mushrooms are available in oriental markets. If fresh mushrooms are not available, use dried, but first soak them in water to cover for 30 minutes or until soft.

In place of salt-reduced soy sauce an additional teaspoon of sake may be used.

Serve spring rolls on a bed of fresh parsley. Accompany with hot mustard and sesame seeds and ketchup and horseradish sauce.

TUNA ANTIPASTO

1   6½-oz. can water-pack tuna, drained
1   15-oz. can artichoke hearts, drained
     and quartered
3   green onions, sliced
¼   pound fresh mushrooms, sliced and
     steamed 3 minutes
1   8-oz. can tomato sauce
1   tablespoon olive oil
¼   cup red wine vinegar
1   clove garlic

Combine ingredients; chill.
Serve with crusty French bread for dipping.

STUFFED MUSHROOMS

1   pound large fresh mushrooms
½   cup oil and vinegar dressing*
     (page 184)
1   bunch fresh spinach
½   cup safflower mayonnaise
2   tablespoons grated onion
1   tablespoon lemon juice
6   ounces of crab meat
½   cup grated low-fat Cheddar cheese

Clean and stem mushrooms; marinate in oil and vinegar dressing for 1 hour. Drain. Wash spinach leaves; shake, but do not dry. Cook covered in heavy skillet 2-3 minutes or until wilted. Drain; squeeze out excess moisture. Chop. Combine mayonnaise, onion and lemon juice. Toss with crab and spinach. Stuff mushrooms; sprinkle with cheese. Bake at 375° for 15 minutes.

Variations: Omit spinach; or omit crab and double the spinach.

CHEESE PIE

1   4-oz. can chopped green chilies
1   lb. low-fat Mozzarella cheese, grated
¾   lb. low-fat Cheddar cheese, grated
1   cup egg substitute, slightly beaten

Place green chilies in a 9-inch pie plate or a quiche pan; top with cheeses. Drizzle with egg substitute. Bake at 425° 35-40 minutes. Remove from oven; let set 10-15 minutes. Cut into squares. Serve at once.

EGGPLANT ANTIPASTO

1 large eggplant
1 8-oz. can tomato sauce
3 cloves garlic, minced
1 green pepper, seeded and chopped
1-2 teaspoons cumin
¼ teaspoon cayenne
1 teaspoon or less salt
1 teaspoon sugar
¼ cup red wine vinegar

Dice unpeeled eggplant; place in a 4-quart sauce pan. Add remaining ingredients. Cover; cook over medium heat 20 minutes, stirring frequently. Uncover; cook 30 minutes or until thick.

Note: Serve hot or cold with tortilla chips* (page 132), crusty French bread or as a vegetable dip. Especially nice on a picnic with roast chicken.

APPETIZER PIZZA

1 1-lb. can tomatoes
2 tablespoons tomato paste
1 tablespoon olive oil
1 loaf French bread
¾ pound Mozzarella or low-fat
    Cheddar cheese, grated

Drain tomatoes; dice. Reserve ½ cup of the juice and mix with diced tomatoes, tomato paste and olive oil. Slice French bread in half lengthwise; spread with sauce and sprinkle with cheese. Bake at 450° 10-15 minutes or until bread is hot and cheese has melted. To serve, slice crosswise into rounds.

TORTILLA CHIPS

corn tortillas

Cut corn tortillas into 8 wedges; place on teflon baking sheet. Bake at 350° about 10 minutes; turn. Bake 10 minutes longer or until crisp.

Variation: Sprinkle with garlic, onion, or chili powder. Serve with tomato salsa* (page 183).

CHEESE TORTILLA CHIPS

4   corn tortillas
½   cup low-fat Cheddar cheese, grated

Cut tortillas into 8 wedges; place on a teflon baking sheet. Bake at 350° about 10 minutes; turn. Bake 10 minutes longer or until crisp. Sprinkle with cheese; bake at 350° 5 minutes or until cheese melts.

Variation: Sprinkle crisp tortilla chips* (see above) with chopped green chilies and dot with tomato salsa* (page 183) before adding cheese. Serve with additional salsa for dipping.

TOMATO SALSA

---

2   cups canned whole tomatoes with
      liquid
4   Jalapeno peppers
1-2 fresh tomatoes, chopped

Cut tomatoes and peppers into 1-inch pieces. Combine all ingredients. Serve chilled or at room temperature.

Variation: Add ½-¾ cup raw or sautéed onion.

ARTICHOKE DIP

---

1   8-oz. can artichoke hearts, drained
      and quartered
1   4-oz. can diced green chilies
2   tablespoons safflower mayonnaise
1½ cups low-fat Cheddar cheese,
      grated

Purée artichoke hearts and green chilies in blender or food processor; stir in mayonnaise. Pour into a shallow baking dish; sprinkle with cheese. Cover; bake in a 350° oven 15 minutes. Uncover; bake 5 minutes or until cheese melts.

Serve with French bread, unsalted tortilla chips* (page 132), sliced cucumbers, zucchini strips, celery sticks, carrot sticks, radishes, or as a stuffing in mushroom caps.

SPINACH DIP

1   cup safflower mayonnaise
1   bunch fresh spinach, chopped
1   cup chopped green onion
1   cup plain low-fat yogurt* (Page 114)
1   teaspoon lemon juice
2-3   drops Tabasco sauce
       ground pepper
1   cup chopped fresh parsley

Put mayonnaise in blender; add spinach and green onion. Whirl 2-3 minutes. Spoon into medium-size bowl; fold in yogurt and remaining ingredients, except parsley. Chill. Just before serving, add parsley.

FRESH LEMONADE

1   cup fresh lemon juice
4   cups cold water
2   tablespoons sugar or lightly to taste
1   lemon, sliced into rings
     orange slices for garnish
     strawberries for garnish
     fresh mint for garnish

Combine lemon juice, water and sugar in a large pitcher; stir to dissolve sugar. Add lemon slices. Chill. Serve over ice. Garnish with orange slices, strawberries and a sprig of fresh mint.

SANGRIA

1   litre red wine
2   fluid ounces brandy
3   fluid ounces fresh orange juice
3   fluid ounces lemon juice
1   cinnamon stick
    sugar to taste
3   oranges with rinds, sliced
3   lemons with rinds, sliced
3   fluid ounces club soda or to taste

Combine all ingredients, except club soda. Chill.
Just before serving, add club soda.

Variation: Add any other fruits in season.

HOT CIDER

1   quart apple juice
2   cloves
1   cinnamon stick

Heat apple juice, cloves and cinnamon over
medium heat until juice is piping hot; do not boil.
Serve at once.

CHOCOLATE WHIP WITH CINNAMON

1   tablespoon cocoa powder
1   cup skim milk
    ground cinnamon
    whipped cream substitute* (page 114)
      (optional)

Mix cocoa powder with 1 tablespoon skim milk to make a paste. Heat remaining milk just to scalding; do not boil. Add cocoa paste; stir. Pour into blender; whirl until frothy. Sprinkle with ground cinnamon. Top with whipped cream substitute.

Variation: For iced chocolate whip, chill and serve over ice.

CAPPUCCINO

    decaffeinated espresso coffee
    skim milk
    cinnamon stick (optional)
    whipped cream substitute* (page 114)

Brew espresso. Heat milk just to scalding; do not boil. Pour milk into blender; whirl until frothy. Fill mugs with ⅓ coffee to ⅔ milk; garnish with cinnamon stick. Top with whipped cream substitute.

Variation: For iced cappucino, chill and serve over ice.

CHAPTER TWELVE

BREADS AND BREAKFASTS

HEALTH BREAD

3 tablespoons dried yeast
½ cup warm water
1½ cups oatmeal
¾ cups coarse ground cracked wheat
2 cups wheat germ
¾ teaspoon or less salt
3 tablespoons safflower oil
3½ cups hot water
¾ cup honey
¼ cup molasses
3 cups whole wheat flour
3 cups unbleached white flour

Dissolve yeast in ½ cup warm water. In large mixing bowl, mix oatmeal, cracked wheat, wheat germ, salt, safflower oil, and hot water. Cool to room temperature. Add honey, molasses, dissolved yeast, whole wheat flour and white flour. Stir with a wooden spoon to form a soft dough. Remove to floured surface. Knead for several minutes, adding more flour as needed to reduce stickiness.

Place dough in a bowl greased with safflower tub margarine. Cover with waxed paper and a kitchen towel. Put in a warm place and let rise until double. Divide dough into 3 loaves and place in loaf pans greased with tub safflower margarine. Cover with waxed paper and a dish towel. Put in a warm place and let rise until double. Bake at 350° for 50 minutes or until bread pulls away from edges of pan. Yield: 3 loaves.

Note: Good toasted or spread with peanut butter.

SOFT PRETZELS

2 teaspoons dried yeast
1½ cups lukewarm water
1 teaspoon salt
3 teaspoons sugar
4 cups flour
1 egg, beaten

Dissolve yeast in water; add salt, sugar and flour. Knead 5-10 minutes, add more flour as necessary to reduce stickiness. Twist dough into shape of cars, trucks, airplanes, animals, flowers, trees, gingerbread boys, numerals or circles. Place on teflon baking sheet. Brush with beaten egg. Bake at 425° 15 minutes or until lightly browned.

CHEESE BREAD

2 cups warm water
4 teaspoons dried yeast
2 tablespoons sugar
1 tablespoon salt
¼ cup safflower oil
6 cups flour
3¼ cups grated low-fat Cheddar cheese

Dissolve yeast in water; add sugar, salt, oil and ½ of the flour. Mix. Add remaining flour; knead into a soft dough — about 5 minutes. Divide dough into 2 loaves; knead 1½ cups of cheese into each loaf. Shape into round loaves; flatten slightly. Bake on a teflon baking sheet or in individual loaf pans at 375° for 30-35 minutes. Makes 2 loaves.

CORN BREAD

¾ cup corn meal
1 cup flour
3 teaspoons baking powder
¾ teaspoon or less salt
¼ cup molasses
¾ cup skim milk
1 egg or ¼ cup egg substitute, beaten
2 tablespoons safflower oil

Sift together corn meal, flour, baking powder and salt; add remaining ingredients. Mix with a spoon. Bake in a 9″-round teflon pan at 375° for 30 minutes.

PANCAKES

1 cup egg substitute
1 cup skim milk
1 cup cold water
2½ cups flour, sifted
¼ cup safflower oil
¾ teaspoon sugar
¼ teaspoon salt

Lightly beat egg substitute, milk and water; add remaining ingredients. Blend with a wire whisk. Bake on a pre-heated teflon griddle. Turn pancakes when top side is bubbly and a few bubbles have broken.

Variation: To make blueberry pancakes, just after bubbles have broken, sprinkle pancakes with blueberries. Turn, brown on other side.

ENERGY BARS

⅔	cup whole wheat flour
⅔	cup safflower oil
1	egg or ¼ cup egg substitute
⅓	cup packed brown sugar
1	teaspoon vanilla
½	teaspoon cinnamon
½	teaspoon baking powder
½	teaspoon or less salt
1½	cups uncooked rolled oats
1	cup unsalted, low-fat Cheddar cheese, grated
¾	cup raisins
1	cup apples, peeled and chopped

Mix flour, oil, egg, sugar, vanilla, cinnamon, baking powder and salt with a wooden spoon; stir in oats, cheese and raisins. Add apples; stir. Drop by heaping tablespoons onto teflon baking sheets. Bake at 375° for 20 minutes or until golden brown. Store in tightly covered jar in refrigerator.

Note: Perfect for breakfast with fresh orange or apple juice.

GRANOLA

3½	cups rolled oats
½	cup sunflower seeds
½	cup unsalted peanuts
½	cup soybeans
¼	cup almonds
¼	cup pecans
¼	cup sesame seeds
¼	cup honey
¼	cup safflower oil
⅛-¼	cup water or more as needed to moisten
½	cup raisins
½	cup dates, dried apples, or dried apricots, chopped

Combine all ingredients, except raisins and dates in a large bowl; toss. Add just enough water to moisten. Pour granola onto a teflon baking sheet. Bake at 300° for 30 minutes or until golden brown, stirring occasionally. Cool. Stir in dates and raisins. Store in covered jar in refrigerator.

CRÊPES

½   cup egg substitute
½   cup skim milk
½   cup cold water
1   cup flour, sifted
2   tablespoons safflower oil
½   teaspoon sugar
⅛   teaspoon salt

Lightly beat egg substitute, milk and water. Add remaining ingredients; blend with a wire whisk. Pour enough batter into a pre-heated, 5-inch teflon crêpe pan to coat bottom of pan; tilt pan to spread batter. Cook 1 minute or just until set. Turn. Cook 1 minute longer or until browned.

Note: Especially good with fresh strawberries and whipped cream substitute* (page 114).

Crêpes may be prepared in advance, layered between was paper, and wrapped in aluminium foil for freezing. Bring to room temperature for easy separation before using. To reheat, remove wax paper layers; wrap in aluminum foil. Heat in a 200° oven for about 10 minutes or until warm.

Some crêpe fillings may be prepared in advance and refrigerated or frozen for later use.

YOGURT PANCAKES

1   cup egg substitute
2   cups plain low-fat yogurt* (page 114)
½   cup flour, sifted
¼   teaspoon salt
1   teaspoon bicarbonate soda

Lightly beat egg substitute; fold in yogurt. Combine dry ingredients; blend with eggs and yogurt using a wire whisk. Bake on a pre-heated teflon griddle, turning when top side is bubbly and a few bubbles have broken.

FRUIT SYRUP

2   cups raspberries, strawberries,
      blackberries or blueberries

Purée fruit in blender. Serve warm or cold over pancakes, waffles, French toast, corn bread, ice cream or sherbet.

Variation: For a sweeter syrup, warm ¼ cup honey with fruit.

For a more tart syrup, add 1 teaspoon lemon juice.

For a thicker syrup, warm fruit and gradually stir in 2 tablespoons corn starch; heat and stir until mixture thickens.

FRENCH OMELET

Select desired fillings per person
- 2 teaspoons chopped onion
- ¼ cup sliced mushrooms
- 1 teaspoon minced green pepper
  wine, broth or water
- 1 teaspoon minced chives
- 2 teaspoons chopped parsley
- 2 teaspoons diced green chilies
- 2 tablespoons crab meat
- 2 tablespoons low-fat Cheddar cheese, grated
- 2 tablespoons chopped tomato

- ¼-½ cup egg substitute per person
- 1 tablespoon water per person
  dash salt
- 1-2 slices tomato per person for garnish
  fresh parsley for garnish

Sauté onion, mushrooms and green pepper until tender in small amount of wine, broth or water.

Beat eggs, water, salt and pepper with a fork until mixture is well-blended, but not frothy. Heat an 8-inch teflon skillet over medium heat until a drop of water sizzles when sprinkled on the pan. Pour in eggs. Tilt pan to spread evenly throughout and at an even depth.

Using a fork, stir rapidly through top of uncooked eggs. Shake pan frequently to keep eggs moving. When egg is set, but still shiny, remove pan from heat. Spoon desired fillings across center. Flip sides of omelet over, envelope style, to hold in filling. Tilt pan and roll omelet over onto plate. Garnish with sliced tomatoes and fresh parsley.

CHAPTER THIRTEEN

SOUPS
AND SANDWICHES

CHICKEN BROTH

1	large chicken
3	quarts cold water
2	stalks celery with leaves
2	carrots, peeled
1	large onion, quartered
2	cloves garlic
¼	teaspoon basil
4	peppercorns
1	tablespoon or less salt
⅛	teaspoon pepper

Put chicken and water in a stock pot. Cover; simmer 2½ hours or until chicken is tender and pulls away from bone. Strain. Remove meat from bones; (freeze for later use). Refrigerate broth overnight; fat will float to the top. Skim and discard fat.

Heat broth to boiling; add vegetables and seasonings. Simmer 2 hours; strain. Reserve vegetables for soup or later use; use broth within 2 weeks or freeze.

Variation: For a richer broth, add another chicken or additional chicken parts.

Note: For maximum economy, when a recipe calls for cooked chicken breasts, buy a whole chicken. Skin and debone breasts. Discard skin. Freeze the bones along with the giblets, necks, wings and backs in a plastic freezer bag. When 5-6 pounds accumulate or when you have a chicken carcass — after a meal of roast chicken — remove bones from freezer bag to a stock pot, add water to cover by 2 inches. Add vegetables and seasonings as in above recipe. Bring to a boil. Cover. Reduce heat. Simmer 5-6 hours. Strain. Discard bones and vegetables as they will be greasy. Refrigerate broth overnight. Skim and discard fat.

CHICKEN SOUP WITH
CHINESE VEGETABLES

1 recipe chicken broth* (page 149)
½ pound fresh mushrooms, sliced
1-2 bunches fresh spinach, torn into
 bite-size pieces
1 cup fresh bean sprouts
2-3 drops hot sauce

Heat chicken broth to boiling. Add mushrooms, then spinach; cook 2 minutes. Add bean sprouts and hot sauce. Serve at once with homemade bread or rolls.

EGG DROP SOUP

4 cups chicken broth* (page 149)
¼ cup egg substitute, beaten
6-8 cherry tomatoes, thinly sliced
4 green onions with tops, thinly
 sliced

Heat chicken broth to boiling. Pour egg through a wire strainer into hot broth. Ladle broth into soup bowls; add 1-2 sliced cherry tomatoes and 1 sliced green onion to each bowl. Serve at once.

TURKEY BROTH

1   turkey carcass with meaty bones
    water to cover (about 3 quarts)
2   cloves garlic
¼   teaspoon basil
4   peppercorns
1   tablespoon or less salt
⅛   teaspoon pepper
4   stalks celery with leaves
4   carrots, peeled
1   large onion, quartered

Place turkey carcass in stock pot; add water to cover. Add seasonings; bring to a boil. Add vegetables. Cover, reduce heat, and simmer 6-8 hours. Strain, discard bones and vegetables as they will be very greasy. Remove meat from bones and reserve for later use. Refrigerate broth overnight. Skim and discard fat which floats to the top. Reheat broth or freeze for later use. Broth will keep up to two weeks in the refrigerator.

HEARTY TURKEY SOUP

1   recipe turkey broth* (see above)
3   carrots, peeled and diced
2   stalks celery, peeled and diced
4   cups cooked pasta or barley
½   pound fresh mushrooms, sliced

Heat broth to boiling; add carrots and celery. Cover; reduce heat and simmer until carrots and celery are tender. Add pasta and mushrooms. Heat.

BEEF BROTH

6 pounds beef bones or 2-3 pounds
   beef shank or short ribs
9 cups water
3 stalks celery with leaves, diced
2 carrots, diced
1 onion, chopped
1 tomato, quartered
2 bay leaves
2 cloves garlic
¼ teaspoon thyme
¼ teaspoon marjoram
8 peppercorns
2 teaspoons salt

Put meat, bones and water in stock pot. Simmer uncovered for 3 hours (do not boil). Strain. Remove any meat or marrow from bones. Add marrow to stock; reserve meat for soup. Chill stock overnight; skim and discard fat which floats to the top. Bring stock to boiling; add remaining ingredients, and simmer uncovered 2 hours. Strain. Reserve vegetables for soup or later use. Use broth within 2 weeks or freeze for later use.

Note: For a hearty soup, do not strain broth. Add 2-3 cups cooked pasta.

BEEF BROTH PARISIAN

═══════════════════════════════════════

    1   leek, finely chopped
    3   cups beef broth* (page 152)
    ½   cup fresh mushrooms, thinly sliced
    ¼   teaspoon tarragon or thyme
    ¼   cup finely chopped fresh parsley

Sauté leek in small amount of broth; add mushrooms and stir over high heat for 1 minute. Add beef broth, tarragon or thyme. Bring to a boil; cover; reduce heat, and simmer 20 minutes. Just before serving, sprinkle with parsley.

MUSHROOM-BARLEY SOUP

═══════════════════════════════════════

    1½   cups barley
    1   recipe beef broth* (page 152)
    ½-¾ pound fresh mushrooms, sliced

Soak barley for several hours or overnight in enough water to cover. Heat broth to boiling, add barley with its soaking liquid. Cover and simmer 2-2½ hours or until barley is tender, add mushrooms. Simmer 10-20 minutes.

MINESTRONE SOUP

1 cup dried white beans
4 cloves garlic, minced
1 medium onion, chopped
2 stalks celery, diced
6 cups chicken broth* (page 149)
1 1-lb. can plum tomatoes
1 tablespoon olive oil
½ cup red wine
1 tablespoon basil
1 tablespoon oregano
  salt to taste
¼ teaspoon pepper
3 medium-size red potatoes, diced
¾ pound fresh green beans, cut
  diagonally into thirds
2 carrots, diced
1½ cups cooked macaroni

Soak white beans for 6 hours in 1 quart of water; pour beans with soaking liquid into a stock pot. Bring to a boil and add garlic, onions and celery. Cook 1½ hours or until beans are tender; add chicken broth, tomatoes, olive oil, wine, basil, oregano, salt and pepper. Heat to boiling; add potatoes in their jackets, green beans and carrots. Reduce heat to simmer; cook 30-45 minutes or until vegetables are tender. Add macaroni.

FRESH TOMATO SOUP

3½	pounds ripe tomatoes, chopped
1	large onion, chopped
1½	teaspoons dill weed
3	tablespoons tomato paste
3	cups beef broth* (page 152)
1½	teaspoons sugar
	ground pepper
2-3	drops Tabasco sauce
	dash salt
2-3	sprigs fresh basil

Combine tomatoes, onion, dill weed and tomato paste in a stock pot. Bring to a boil, stirring often; reduce heat, cover and simmer 15 minutes. Cool to room temperature. Pour into blender or food processor; whirl until smooth. Return to stock pot; add remaining ingredients. Heat to serving temperature.

Variation: Add 1 cup cooked macaroni.

GAZPACHO

1 fresh ripe tomato
1 green pepper
3 stalks celery
1 cucumber
1 small onion
3 tablespoons parsley
4 green onions
2 cloves garlic
¼ cup red wine vinegar
3 tablespoons safflower oil
1 tablespoon olive oil
½ teaspoon salt
6 cups canned tomatoes, chopped
¼ teaspoon horseradish

Combine all ingredients except horseradish; purée in blender. Chill at least 3 hours. Just before serving, stir in horseradish.

MEXICAN CHILI SOUP

  4   cups chicken broth* (page 149)
  1   28-oz. can plum tomatoes
  1   small onion, diced
  1   clove garlic, crushed
  1   4-oz. can diced green chilies
  1   1-lb. can pinto beans
  1   15-oz. can garbanzo beans
 1½   cups cooked chicken, diced
  2   cups cooked macaroni

Heat chicken broth and tomatoes just to boiling; immediately reduce heat. Add onion, garlic and green chilies; simmer 1 hour. Add beans, chicken and macaroni; simmer 20 minutes.

Note: Serve with corn tortillas.

CREAM OF ASPARAGUS SOUP

  2   cups chopped asparagus
  3   tablespoons chopped onion
  1   recipe cream of chicken soup*
         (page 158)

Steam asparagus and onion; purée in blender. Heat cream of chicken soup gradually over low heat; add asparagus and onion. Heat to serving temperature.

CREAM OF CHICKEN SOUP

2 cups chicken broth* (page 149)
¾ cup grated raw potato

Heat chicken broth to boiling; gradually add grated potato. Simmer 10-25 minutes, stirring frequently until potato is tender and broth has thickened. Pour into blender and purée. Keeps several days in refrigerator.

Variation: As a thickener in place of potato, shake ¼ cup flour and ½ cup water in a covered jar to form a smooth paste; gradually add to boiling broth, stirring constantly until broth has thickened.

HEARTY CREAM OF CHICKEN SOUP

1 recipe cream of chicken soup* (see above)
½ cup chicken broth* (page 149)
2 carrots, cooked and diced
2 red potatoes with skins, cooked and diced

Heat cream of chicken soup over low heat; add remaining ingredients and heat to serving temperature.

CREAM OF CELERY SOUP

2 cups chopped celery with leaves
3 tablespoons chopped onion
1 recipe cream of chicken soup*
   (page 158)

Sauté celery and onion in water or small amount of broth until tender. Purée in blender; add to cream of chicken soup; heat to serving temperature.

CREAM OF CUCUMBER SOUP

1½ medium cucumbers, peeled
1 clove garlic
3 tablespoons chopped fresh parsley
1½ tablespoons onion
½ cup chicken broth* (page 149)
1½ tablespoons white wine vinegar
1 cup plain low-fat yogurt* (page 114)

Purée cucumbers, garlic, parsley, and onion in blender; add broth and vinegar. Fold in yogurt. Cover and chill 2 hours. Will keep up to 24 hours in refrigerator.

Variation: Garnish with croutons, sliced green onions, parsley, fresh mint, chopped tomatoes or sunflower seeds.

Note: Refreshing on a hot afternoon.

CREAM OF MUSHROOM SOUP

2 cups beef broth* (page 152)
1 cup grated raw potato
1½ cups diced mushrooms
⅛ teaspoon pepper

Heat broth to boiling; gradually add grated raw potato. Simmer 10-25 minutes, stirring frequently until potato is tender and broth has thickened. Pour into blender and purée. Return to saucepan; add mushrooms. Season. Simmer 15 minutes.

CREAM OF ZUCCHINI SOUP

1½ pounds zucchini, sliced
¼ cup chopped onion
¾ cup water
1 teaspoon or less salt
½ teaspoon sugar
½ teaspoon basil
¼ cup flour
2 cups skim milk
chopped fresh parsley for garnish

Bring zucchini, onion, water, salt, sugar, and basil to a boil; cover and simmer 15 minutes or until onion is tender. Purée in blender. Return to stock pot. Shake flour and water in a covered jar to form a smooth paste; slowly whisk into zucchini. Heat to serving temperature over low heat. Serve at once or refrigerate until ready to serve.

SANDWICHES

When preparing sandwiches, be creative.

Try a variety of breads, serve breads toasted, untoasted or open-faced, top with lettuce, tomato, onion, sprouts, green peppers, mushrooms, safflower mayonnaise and mustard and garnish with fresh fruits of the season.

CHICKEN SANDWICH FILLING

1   cup cooked chicken, finely chopped
½   cup finely chopped celery
¼   cup finely chopped almonds or
      waterchestnuts
⅓   cup safflower mayonnaise

Combine ingredients in medium bowl. Toss.

CLUB HOUSE SANDWICH

3   slices toast per sandwich
    lettuce leaves
    cooked chicken breast, sliced
    safflower mayonnaise
    sliced tomato

Top first slice of toast with lettuce, chicken and mayonnaise. Top with second slice of toast; add tomato slices and top with third slice of toast. Slice diagonally into quarters.

TUNA SANDWICH FILLING

½   teaspoon fresh lemon juice
1   6½-oz. can water pack tuna,
    drained
3   tablespoons minced onion
2   tablespoons minced celery
2   tablespoons waterchestnuts, finely
    chopped
⅓   cup safflower mayonnaise
    dash prepared mustard (optional)

Sprinkle lemon juice over tuna; toss with onion, celery and waterchestnuts. Moisten with mayonnaise. Mix with mustard.

CHAPTER FOURTEEN

SALADS AND
SALAD DRESSINGS

SALAD OF TOMATOES, MOZZARELLA AND BASIL

3 large ripe tomatoes
¾ pound Mozzarella cheese
3 teaspoons fresh basil
2 tablespoons fresh lemon juice
⅓ cup olive oil
    fresh spinach leaves
    ground black pepper

Cut tomatoes in half; slice each half into 3 wedges. Cut cheese into 1-inch cubes. Mix basil with lemon juice and olive oil; pour just enough over spinach to moisten. Arrange spinach on chilled salad plates. Toss cheese and tomatoes with remaining dressing; arrange over spinach. Sprinkle with black pepper.

Note: To use fresh basil, rather than dried, double the amount and omit the lemon juice.

TOMATO AND CUCUMBER SALAD

½ cup safflower mayonnaise
½ teaspoon finely chopped white
    onion
1 large ripe tomato
1 medium cucumber, peeled and
    diced
    lettuce greens
    ground black pepper

Combine mayonnaise and onion; toss with tomato and cucumber. Serve over lettuce. Sprinkle with freshly ground pepper.

TOMATOES VINAIGRETTE

⅓ cup safflower oil
2½ tablespoons olive oil
2½ tablespoons red wine vinegar
¼ teaspoon or less salt
1 clove garlic, minced
¼ teaspoon pepper
¼ teaspoon dry mustard
¾ teaspoon oregano
3 large ripe tomatoes
1 tablespoon finely chopped fresh
    parsley
2 tablespoons finely chopped onion
    salad greens

Combine safflower oil, olive oil, vinegar and seasonings; pour over tomatoes. Refrigerate 3-4 hours or overnight. Just before serving, drain off some of the dressing and toss with the salad greens. Place on chilled salad plates. Toss parsley and onion with tomatoes; arrange over greens.

SALAD OF FRESH MUSHROOMS AND WATERCHESTNUTS

½ pound fresh mushrooms, sliced
1 8-oz. can sliced waterchestnuts,
    drained
2 tablespoons chopped green onion
3 tablespoons fresh lemon juice
5 tablespoons olive oil
    salt and pepper to taste

Combine all ingredients in a glass salad bowl; let stand 20 minutes. Serve.

CUCUMBER AND ONION SALAD

 1 cucumber, peeled and thinly sliced
 ¾ teaspoon salt (to be rinsed off)
 ½ cup plain low-fat yogurt* (page 114)
 2 tablespoons cider vinegar
 ⅛ teaspoon sugar
 1 small white onion, halved and cut into
     rings
 2-3 drops Tabasco sauce

Sprinkle cucumber with salt; let stand 30 minutes.
Rinse; drain and pat dry. Combine yogurt, vinegar
and sugar; pour over cucumbers and onion. Chill
30-60 minutes. Sprinkle with Tabasco sauce.

Variation: Sprinkle with dill seed.

SALAD OF GREEN BEANS, TOMATOES,
ARTICHOKES AND MUSHROOMS

 1 pound fresh green beans, cooked
 1 15-oz. can artichoke hearts
 1 6-oz. can sliced waterchestnuts
 ½ pound fresh mushrooms, steamed
     2-3 minutes, sliced
     dressing of oil and vinegar with
       lemon* (page 184)
 15 cherry tomatoes, chilled

Drain beans, artichokes, waterchestnuts, and
mushrooms. Chill. Just before serving, moisten
with dressing; toss with chilled tomatoes.

ZUCCHINI SALAD

2 small zucchini, peeled and sliced
  lengthwise into julienne strips
  Dijon vinaigrette* (page 183)
  bibb or iceberg lettuce leaves
3 cherry tomatoes, halved, for
  garnish

Toss zucchini with vinaigrette. Line a salad bowl with lettuce; fill with zucchini. Garnish.

ZUCCHINI STUFFED WITH CRAB

4 medium zucchini
2 cups dry white wine
¼ pound fresh mushrooms, sliced
1 teaspoon lemon juice
1 tablespoon grated onion
6 ounces of crab meat
8 artichoke hearts, halved and chilled
½ cup safflower mayonnaise
  cherry tomatoes for garnish

Cut zucchini in half lengthwise; hollow centers by scraping and removing seeds with a spoon. Poach zucchini in wine just until tender, add mushrooms during the final 3 minutes of cooking; drain, sprinkle with lemon juice and chill. Combine mushrooms, onions, crab, artichokes and mayonnaise; chill. Spoon into zucchini boats. Serve on crisp lettuce greens. Garnish with cherry tomatoes.

Variation: Substitute chicken or water-pack tuna for crab.

CRAB STUFFED PEPPERS

    1   cup crab meat
    1   teaspoon minced onion
    1   teaspoon lemon juice
    1   cup finely chopped celery
  3-4   green peppers
        safflower mayonnaise to moisten
   ¾   cup hearts of lettuce, diced

Combine crab meat, onion, lemon juice and celery. Chill. Remove tops from green peppers; hollow out insides. Just before serving, toss mayonnaise and lettuce with crab mixture; spoon into green peppers.

Variation: Chicken or salmon may be substituted for crab. Tomatoes may be substituted for peppers.

STUFFED ARTICHOKE SALAD

2   fresh artichokes, cooked
1   cup crab meat
3   tablespoons chopped green pepper
2   tablespoons finely chopped onion
1   teaspoon lemon juice
¼   cup safflower mayonnaise
½   cup grated low-fat Cheddar cheese
    tomato slices for garnish

Remove small center leaves of each artichoke, leaving a cup; carefully remove choke. Toss crab meat, green pepper, onion, lemon juice, mayonnaise and cheese; stuff artichokes. Place in baking dish; add water — just to cover bottom of dish. Cover and bake at 375° 35 minutes or until hot. Garnish with tomato slices.

Note: This is also delicious cold. To serve cold, chill ingredients. Fill artichokes just before serving.

Variation: Cooked chicken may be substituted for crab.

CRAB LOUIS

1   head lettuce
½   pound crab meat
¼   cup sliced waterchestnuts
2   stalks celery, thinly sliced
3   green onions with tops, thinly
      sliced
½   green pepper, chopped
2   tomatoes, cut into wedges
1   bunch asparagus spears, steamed
      2-4 minutes
     lemon wedges

Dressing:
¾   cup safflower mayonnaise
2   tablespoons lemon juice
2   tablespoons grated onion

Combine mayonnaise, lemon juice and onion; chill 30 minutes. Line chilled salad bowls with outside leaves of lettuce; shred remaining lettuce. Toss shredded lettuce, crab, waterchestnuts, celery, green onion and green pepper with dressing to moisten; spoon into lettuce-lined bowls. Garnish with tomatoes, asparagus and lemon wedges.

SALAD NICOISE

3	red potatoes, cooked *al dente*, and thinly sliced
½-¾	pound fresh green beans, cooked *al dente*, and sliced diagonally into thirds
8-10	artichoke hearts, quartered
3	carrots, cooked *al dente*, and thinly sliced
½	white onion, thinly sliced and separated into rings
½	green pepper, cut into rings
½	red pepper, cut into rings
1	bunch leaf lettuce, torn into bite-size pieces
1-2	cans water-packed tuna fish, drained and flaked
1½	tablespoons chopped fresh parsley ground pepper
6-8	cherry or plum tomatoes, halved

Dressing:

½	cup olive oil
½	cup safflower oil
¼	cup tarragon-flavored vinegar
2	tablespoons fresh lemon juice
1	clove garlic, chopped
1½	teaspoons dry mustard
¾	teaspoon or less salt
½	teaspoon pepper

Combine ingredients for dressing; pour over vegetables. Chill 3-4 hours, stirring often. Arrange lettuce on a medium tray; mound tuna in center. Drain vegetables, reserving dressing, and arrange in piles around tuna. Sprinkle with parsley and ground pepper. Garnish with tomatoes. Drizzle with reserved dressing.

HOT TUNA SALAD

2   cans water-packed tuna, drained
3   stalks celery, thinly sliced
½   green pepper, chopped
½   cup waterchestnuts, sliced
1   tablespoon fresh lemon juice
1   tablespoon grated onion
⅔   cup safflower mayonnaise
2   cups grated low-fat Cheddar cheese
½   cup crushed corn flakes (optional)

Combine ingredients except cheese and corn flakes. Place in individual baking shells. Broil 10 minutes or until hot. Top with cheese; sprinkle with corn flakes. Bake 3-5 minutes or until cheese melts.

Variation: Chicken may be substituted for tuna fish and Mozzarella cheese for Cheddar.

CHICKEN SALAD

2   teaspoons lemon juice
2   cooked chicken breasts, cubed
2   stalks celery, diced
¼   cup slivered almonds
    safflower mayonnaise
    salt and pepper to taste
4   small tomatoes or green peppers
    fresh spinach greens

Squeeze lemon juice over chicken, add celery and almonds; toss. Moisten with mayonnaise. Season. Cut tops from tomatoes; hollow out centers and fill with chicken. Serve on spinach-lined plates.

TACO SALAD

1   pound extra-lean ground round
1   onion, chopped
2   tomatoes, chopped
1   head lettuce
2   cups grated low-fat Cheddar cheese
    tortilla chips* (page 132)
    plain non-fat yogurt* (page 114)
    tomato salsa* (page 183)

Brown ground round with onion; drain. Toss with tomatoes. Line salad bowls with outside leaves of lettuce; shred remaining lettuce and add to bowls. Cover with ground round and tomatoes. Top with cheese. Line rim of bowl with chips. Pass with yogurt and salsa.

Note: One package unsalted, baked in safflower oil, taco chips may be used in place of homemade chips.

SUPER TACO SALAD

1	1-lb. can tomatoes with liquid
¼	teaspoon or less salt
¾	teaspoon dry mustard
1¼	teaspoons chili powder
1	small clove garlic, minced
¾	pound cooked chicken breast, cubed
1	1-lb. can kidney beans with liquid or 1½ cups homecooked kidney beans plus ½ cup liquid
½	head lettuce, chopped
1	medium onion, chopped
2	cups low-fat Cheddar or Mozzarella cheese, grated
	tortilla chips* (page 132)
	tomato salsa* (page 183) optional
	plain low-fat yogurt* (page 114) (optional)

Combine tomatoes, salt, mustard, chili powder and garlic; heat just to boiling. Reduce heat and simmer 5 minutes; add chicken. Simmer 5 more minutes; add kidney beans. Heat. Spoon into bowls. Top with lettuce, onion, cheese, tortilla chips, salsa and yogurt, as desired.

Note: Prepare tortilla chips according to instructions in appetizer section or use 1 package unsalted, baked in safflower oil, taco chips.

Variation: Substitute 1-lb. extra lean ground round for chicken.

POTATO SALAD

4 new potatoes, with skins, cooked and diced
¾ cup chopped white onion
1½ cups finely chopped celery
½ green pepper, chopped
½ cup chopped green onion
1 8-oz. can sliced waterchestnuts, drained
1 tablespoon prepared mustard
¾ cup safflower mayonnaise
½ teaspoon or less salt
¼ teaspoon pepper
¼ teaspoon dill weed
1 tablespoon finely chopped parsley

Toss potatoes, onion, celery, green pepper, green onion, and waterchestnuts; chill. Combine mustard, mayonnaise, salt, pepper, dill weed, and parsley; chill. One hour before serving, toss potatoes and vegetables with dressing (use dressing sparingly, just to moisten).

CURRIED POTATO SALAD

2 pounds new potatoes
1 cup safflower mayonnaise
1 tablespoon lemon juice
¼ teaspoon curry powder

Steam potatoes, drain, peel and slice. Blend mayonnaise, lemon juice and curry. Fold in potatoes. Chill and serve.

MACARONI SALAD

═══════════════════════════

¾	cup safflower mayonnaise
1	tablespoon prepared mustard
1	tablespoon cider vinegar
1	tablespoon safflower oil
⅓	teaspoon or less salt
¼	teaspoon pepper
¼	teaspoon dill weed
1	tablespoon finely chopped parsley
2½	cups cooked macaroni
¾	cup chopped white onion
½	cup chopped green onion
1½	cups finely chopped celery

Combine mayonnaise, mustard, vinegar, oil, salt, pepper, dill weed and parsley; pour over macaroni, onions and celery. Toss. Chill several hours.

THREE BEAN SALAD

¾ lb. green beans, cooked, drained and
    sliced on the diagonal into thirds
2 cups cooked kidney beans
1 8-oz. can garbanzo beans, drained
1 white onion, chopped
1 green pepper, chopped
2-3 stalks celery, chopped
    pinch sugar
1 recipe dressing of oil and vinegar*
    (page 184)

Toss beans with onion, green pepper and celery. Set aside. Add sugar to oil and vinegar dressing; pour over vegetables and toss. Chill 3-4 hours.

Note: A 1-lb. can of cut green beans and a 1-lb. can of kidney beans may be used in place of the fresh.

COLESLAW

½ cup safflower mayonnaise
2 tablespoons rice vinegar
1 teaspoon Dijon mustard
½ head cabbage, shredded
½ green pepper, finely chopped
½ white onion, finely chopped

Combine mayonnaise, vinegar and mustard. Chill. Just before serving, toss cabbage, green pepper and onion; moisten with dressing.

WATERMELON SALAD

1   watermelon
1   honeydew melon
1   cantaloupe
2   pounds grapes
1   quart strawberries
1   quart raspberries
1   quart blueberries
    fresh mint for garnish

Pick a rolly-polly watermelon. Cut lengthwise from each end, toward center, slicing off top third. Leave a center portion 2½″ wide for the handle. Using a serrated knife, make big scallops around the top edge of the watermelon.

With a melon baller, form balls from watermelon, honeydew and cantaloupe. Toss with grapes and berries. Scrape inside of watermelon with a spoon to remove excess melon. Fill with fruit. Tie a bow on the basket handle to coordinate with table setting and napkins. Garnish with fresh mint. Serves 8-10.

Note: At the end of the meal, rinse watermelon basket; pat dry and freeze for later use.

SUMMER SALAD

━━━━━━━━━━━━━━━━━━━━━━━━━━━━━

 ¼ watermelon
 ½ cantaloupe
 ½ honeydew melon
 1 pound grapes
 1 pint strawberries
 1 pint raspberries
 1 pint cherries
 1 pint blueberries

Remove rind from melons. Slice melons into
wedges. Stem grapes. Hull strawberries. Pile
strawberries in the center of a large basket or tray;
surround with watermelon, honeydew, cantaloupe, raspberries and cherries. Garnish with
grapes and blueberries. Serves 8-10.

CRANBERRY RELISH

━━━━━━━━━━━━━━━━━━━━━━━━━━━━━

 1 pound (4 cups) fresh cranberries
 2 oranges, cut into eighths
 2 red delicious apples, cut into eighths
 ⅓ cup sugar or to taste

Wash cranberries (discard any that are soft or
blemished). Wash oranges; do not peel. Put cranberries, apples, and oranges through medium
blade of a grinder or food processor. Drain off
excess juice; reserve. Add sugar; stir. Pour ½-¾
of the reserved juice into the relish (relish should
be very moist, but not runny). Chill 24 hours.
Keeps 2-3 weeks. Yields 2 quarts.

WINTER SALAD

3   oranges
2   satsumas or tangerines
½   pound black grapes
1   papaya
1   fresh pineapple
2   bananas — dip in lemon juice;
        sprinkle with walnuts
10 figs
10 dates
2   apples — dip in lemon juice
1   cup frozen blueberries for garnish

Peel oranges and tangerines; divide into segments and remove skin and membranes. Stem grapes. Cut papaya in half; scrape seeds. Carefully cut out pulp, leaving shell intact. Slice pulp and return to papaya boat. Lay pineapple on its side. Slice off upper ⅓, leaving stem intact. Using a curved grapefruit knife, remove pineapple from shell; cut into spears. Return to pineapple boat.

To serve: Place pineapple boat in center of a large basket or tray. Position papaya boats on each side. Surround with remaining fruits. Garnish with blueberries. Serves 8-10.

Helpful Hint: To freeze strawberries, raspberries, blueberries or blackberries, wash berries; pat dry. Place in a single layer on a baking sheet. Freeze 2–3 hours. Remove from freezer and quickly place in covered freezer containers. Return to freezer. Berries will not stick together and may be removed individually as needed for garnish. They may also be puréed and used on bread or toast in place of jam.

SAFFLOWER MAYONNAISE

1 egg
1 teaspoon red wine vinegar
2 teaspoons fresh lemon juice
1 teaspoon Dijon mustard
½ teaspoon or less salt
¼ cup olive oil
1¼ cups safflower oil

Combine first six ingredients in blender; whirl. With machine running, add safflower oil, one tablespoon at a time. Refrigerate. Keeps several weeks. Yield: 1½ cups.

Variation: To make herbed mayonnaise, add ½ teaspoon basil, dill, tarragon or parsley just before serving.

PRIMAVERA DRESSING

⅓ cup safflower oil
¼ cup olive oil
¼ cup cider vinegar
½ teaspoon Dijon mustard
salt to taste
pepper to taste

Combine oils, vinegar, and mustard in covered jar; shake. Drizzle over salad greens. Season to taste.

DIJON VINAIGRETTE

4   tablespoons Dijon mustard
3   tablespoons red wine vinegar
1   tablespoon white wine vinegar
¼   teaspoon salt
1-2 cloves garlic
½   teaspoon basil
⅛   teaspoon black pepper
2   drops hot sauce
1   tablespoon grated onion
12 tablespoons safflower oil

Combine mustard and vinegar in blender. Add salt, garlic, basil, black pepper, hot sauce and onion; whirl. With machine running, add oil, one tablespoon at a time. Chill. Keeps several weeks. Yield: 1¼ cups.

TOMATO SALSA

4   whole Jalapeno peppers
1-2 fresh tomatoes, chopped
1   1-lb. can plum tomatoes with liquid
¼   teaspoon cumin (optional)
¼   teaspoon cayenne (optional)

Dice peppers, fresh tomatoes and canned tomatoes into 1-inch pieces. Combine in covered jar. Chill. Season.

Variation: For a hotter sauce, add Tabasco sauce to taste.

Note: Great as a salad dressing or as a dip.

DRESSING OF OIL AND VINEGAR

½ cup safflower oil
¼ cup olive oil
¼ cup cider vinegar
¼ teaspoon pepper

Combine ingredients in covered jar; shake. Yield: 1 cup.

Variation: To make creamy Italian dressing, add ⅓ cup safflower mayonnaise.

DRESSING OF OIL AND VINEGAR WITH LEMON

½ cup safflower oil
¼ cup cider vinegar
3 tablespoons fresh lemon juice
dash pepper
1 clove garlic

Combine ingredients in a covered jar; shake. Yield: 1 cup.

Variation: Substitute olive oil for safflower oil or add ¼-½ teaspoon dry mustard powder.

GARLIC FRENCH DRESSING

⅓   cup safflower oil
⅓   cup olive oil
2½ teaspoons cider vinegar
¼   teaspoon dry mustard
4   cloves garlic
    salt and pepper to taste

Combine ingredients in covered jar; shake. Let set 3-4 days before using. Drizzle over salad greens. Season with salt and liberally with pepper. Yield: ¾ cup.

CREAMY FRENCH DRESSING

½   cup safflower mayonnaise
1   tablespoon cider vinegar
1   tablespoon skim milk
½   teaspoon paprika
¼   teaspoon dry mustard

Combine ingredients in medium bowl; beat with wire whisk. Chill

THOUSAND ISLAND DRESSING

½   cup ketchup
¼   cup safflower mayonnaise
1   tablespoon minced green pepper

Combine ketchup and mayonnaise. Chill. Stir in green pepper.

YOGURT DRESSING

1   cup safflower mayonnaise
½   cup plain low-fat yogurt* (page 114)
3   tablespoons chopped green onion
¼   cup dried parsley
2   tablespoons tarragon vinegar
2   tablespoons lemon juice
1   clove garlic, minced
⅛   teaspoon pepper

Combine ingredients with wire whisk. Chill 3 hours.

CHAPTER FIFTEEN

VEGETABLES

NOTES ON COOKING VEGETABLES: There is no more heart-healthy fare than vegetables. To preserve the natural sugars and nutrients of vegetables do not wash them until just prior to cooking. The most important rule about cooking vegetables is not to overcook — cook until just crisp-tender and still very colorful.

TO STEAM VEGETABLES: Bring 1-2 inches of water to a boil in a medium saucepan. Place vegetables in a steamer basket and place the basket over the boiling water. Cover saucepan with a tight fitting lid. Steam until vegetables are crisp-tender and still very colorful.

TO BOIL VEGETABLES: Bring a small amount of water or broth to a boil — use the smallest amount possible. Add vegetables; bring to a second boil. Cover; reduce heat. Cook at a gentle boil until crisp-tender and rich in color.

TO COOK FROZEN VEGETABLES: Follow package directions; omit salt.

TO STIR-FRY VEGETABLES: Slice vegetables to a uniform thickness of about ⅛th of an inch. Heat a small amount of chicken broth* (page 149) or beef broth* (page 152) in a wok or heavy skillet over high heat. Add vegetables requiring longest cooking time first; gradually add remaining vegetables. Stir rapidly with long chopsticks or flat wooden spoon until vegetables show signs of wilting slightly. Lower heat. Cover with lid — leave on only briefly, just until vegetables are crisp-tender. Serve at once.

TO OVEN-ROAST VEGETABLES: Pare and quarter such vegetables as potatoes, celery, carrots, onions and green peppers. Place on rack in baking dish; add ½ cup water, wine or broth. Cover. Steam 30-40 minutes or until tender. If using mushrooms, tomatoes or artichoke hearts, they should be added the last 15 minutes.

TO MICROWAVE VEGETABLES: Vegetables cooked in the microwave retain their bright color and freshness as well as their vitamins and minerals since they are usually cooked with little or no additional water. For correct cooking procedure and timing for individual vegetables, consult a microwave manual.

TO BLANCH VEGETABLES: Bring 1-2 inches of water to a boil in a medium saucepan. Place vegetables in a steamer basket and place the basket over the boiling water. Cover saucepan with a tight fitting lid. Reduce normal cooking time by ¾. For example, normal cooking time for fresh peas is 3-5 minutes, so the blanching time would be 45-80 seconds — at this point vegetables will be rich in color and translucent. Immediately plunge vegetables into ice water to stop additional cooking. Consult a vegetable blanching and freezing chart for blanching times for individual vegetables.

FRESH ARTICHOKES

2-3 fresh artichokes
3 tablespoons chopped onion
3 cloves garlic
1½ cups dry white wine
2 tablespoons olive oil
¼ cup safflower oil
dash salt
⅛ teaspoon pepper
1 lemon, sliced

Wash artichokes. Cut 1-inch off of top; cut off stem and tips of leaves. Brush cut edges with lemon juice. Combine remaining ingredients. Bring to a boil. Place artichokes upright in mixture; cover and simmer until bottom leaves pull off easily. Drain. Serve hot or cold with homemade safflower mayonnaise* (page 182) or Dijon vinaigrette* (page 183).

Note: Artichokes are delicious cooked in the microwave. Follow the recipe Fresh Artichokes With Lemon* (page 126).

ARTICHOKE HEARTS WITH LEMON, GARLIC AND OLIVE OIL

fresh artichoke hearts
fresh lemon juice
cloves garlic
olive oil
black pepper

Cook artichokes. Remove hearts; quarter. Squeeze lemon juice over. Set aside. Heat garlic and enough olive oil to cover artichokes; pour over artichokes. Toss gently to coat. Sprinkle with black pepper.

FRESH ASPARAGUS WITH LEMON

1   pound fresh asparagus
    juice of ½ lemon

Wash asparagus; snap stalks. Place on vegetable steamer rack over boiling water; cover and steam 5-6 minutes — just until barely tender.

To microwave, arrange asparagus in a single layer, tender tips toward center, in a microwave-proof baking dish; cover with plastic wrap, prick with a fork to allow steam to escape. Cook 3-4 minutes — just until barely tender. Drizzle with lemon juice.

Variation: Omit lemon juice. Serve with homemade safflower mayonnaise* (page 182) or Dijon vinaigrette* (page 183).

CELERY REMOULADE

1   pound fresh celery root
1   recipe Dijon vinaigrette* (page 183)
    fresh parsley
    ripe tomatoes, sliced into wedges

Steam celery root until tender; drain. Toss with just enough Dijon vinaigrette to moisten. Chill 2-3 hours. Garnish with fresh parsley and ripe tomatoes.

GREEN BEANS WITH FRESH LEMON AND TARRAGON

¾   pound fresh green beans
⅓   cup safflower oil
3   tablespoons olive oil
½   cup fresh lemon juice
2   cloves garlic, minced
1   teaspoon dried tarragon or
     1 tablespoon fresh tarragon
1   teaspoon oregano
⅛   teaspoon salt
⅛   teaspoon black pepper

Wash beans; remove ends and strings. Place in vegetable steamer rack over boiling water; steam 15-25 minutes or until tender. Combine remaining ingredients; pour over cooked beans. Serve hot or cold.

GREEN BEANS, ITALIAN STYLE

1   pound fresh green beans
½   cup chicken broth* (page 149)
2   tablespoons safflower oil
2   cups canned plum tomatoes
    dash oregano
    salt to taste
    pepper to taste

Wash beans. Remove ends and strings; cut on the diagonal into 1-inch pieces. Set aside. Combine remaining ingredients and bring to a boil. Add beans; cook covered 15-25 minutes or until beans are tender.

GREEN BEANS WITH MUSHROOMS AND WATERCHESTNUTS

¾   pound fresh green beans
½   pound fresh mushrooms, sliced
1   8-oz. can sliced waterchestnuts
2   tablespoons lemon juice
¼   teaspoon or less salt
⅛   teaspoon pepper

Place beans in a vegetable steamer over boiling water; cook 15-25 minutes or until beans are nearly tender. Add mushrooms the last 5 minutes, add waterchestnuts the last 3 minutes. Spoon beans into serving bowl; toss with lemon juice, salt and pepper.

STIR-FRIED BROCCOLI

1   large bunch broccoli
½   cup chicken broth* (page 149)
1   teaspoon sesame oil
2   teaspoons cornstarch
2   tablespoons water
3   tablespoons sesame seeds

Wash broccoli; cut flowerets from stems and set aside. Peel stems; cut diagonally into ¼-inch pieces. Heat chicken broth and sesame oil in wok or heavy skillet. Stir-fry stems 2 minutes; add flowerets, stir-fry 2 more minutes. Add cornstarch dissolved in 2 tablespoons water and toss quickly to coat and glaze broccoli. Sprinkle with sesame seeds.

DIJON VEGETABLES

    broccoli flowerets
    cauliflower flowerets
    cherry tomatoes, halved
1   recipe Dijon vinaigrette* (page 183)
    poppy seeds

Steam broccoli and cauliflower until barely tender. Chill. Toss tomatoes and cauliflower in just enough vinaigrette to moisten. Chill 4-6 hours. Just before serving, lightly coat broccoli with vinaigrette. Place tomatoes and cauliflower in serving bowl; ring with broccoli. Sprinkle with poppy seeds.

NIPPY CARROTS

1   bunch fresh carrots, peeled
½   cup chicken broth* (page 149)
    tub safflower margarine
1½ teaspoons horseradish
½   cup safflower mayonnaise
    ground pepper
¼   cup bread crumbs

Slice carrots diagonally into ¼-inch pieces. Cook in chicken broth until crisp-tender; drain, reserving ¼ cup broth — add more chicken broth if necessary to get ¼ cup. Grease an ovenproof dish with tub safflower margarine; add carrots. Mix broth, horseradish, mayonnaise, and pepper; spread over carrots. Top with bread crumbs. Bake at 375° for 15 minutes

Variation: In place of carrots and black pepper, use 1 large bunch fresh spinach greens and ½ teaspoon nutmeg.

CORN ON THE COB

=================================

    fresh corn
    fresh lemons
    ground pepper

Husk corn; remove silks. Place on vegetable
steamer rack over boiling water; cover and steam
6-8 minutes.

To microwave, place ears in oblong microwave
dish; cover with wax paper. Cook 4-6 minutes for
2 ears; 7-8 minutes for 4 ears. Turn once during
cooking time.

Squeeze fresh lemon juice over corn. Sprinkle
with ground pepper.

Variation: Sprinkle with garlic powder, onion powder, chili powder or black pepper.

BARBECUED EGGPLANT

=================================

    1   medium eggplant, unpeeled
    ⅓   cup olive oil
    2   tablespoons tarragon white wine
          vinegar
    1   clove garlic, minced
    ⅛   teaspoon or less salt
    ¼   teaspoon oregano

Cut eggplant lengthwise into 8 wedges. Combine
oil, vinegar, garlic, salt and oregano in a covered
jar; shake. Pour over eggplant. Drain excess oil.
Grill eggplant slices over hot coals until tender,
turning once.

BAKED EGGPLANT

1   medium onion, chopped
1   clove garlic, minced
2   tablespoons red wine
1   1-lb. can plum tomatoes
1   8-oz. can tomato sauce
⅓   cup tomato paste
2   teaspoons oregano
½   pound fresh mushrooms, sliced
1   medium eggplant
⅓   cup flour
1   cup egg substitute, beaten
1   cup bread crumbs
8   oz. Mozzarella cheese, sliced

Sauté onion and garlic in red wine until tender; add tomatoes, tomato sauce, tomato paste, oregano and mushrooms. Bring to a boil; reduce heat and simmer uncovered for 30 minutes.

Cut eggplant crosswise into ¼-inch slices; coat with flour. Dip into egg substitute, then into bread crumbs. Cook in a teflon skillet until lightly browned, turning once.

In the bottom of a 13x9x2-inch baking dish, spread ½ of the tomato mixture, layer half of the eggplant slices, top with cheese and spread with sauce. Repeat layers. Pour remaining sauce over top. Bake uncovered at 350° for 20-30 minutes.

RATATOUILLE

1   medium eggplant, cut into 1-inch
      cubes
1   large onion, sliced into rings
3   medium zucchini, cut into ½-inch
      slices
2   green peppers, seeded and cut into
      ½-inch pieces
3   large tomatoes, chopped
1   cup minced fresh parsley
½   teaspoon salt
1   tablespoon fresh basil or ½ teaspoon
      dried basil
4   cloves garlic, pressed
2   tablespoons olive oil
2   tablespoons safflower oil
     ground pepper to taste

Layer vegetables in a deep casserole; sprinkle with parsley, salt, basil and garlic. Drizzle with olive and safflower oil. Chill overnight. Bake covered in a 350° oven for 3 hours. Sprinkle with ground pepper. Serve.

STIR-FRIED VEGETABLES

chicken broth* (page 149)
onions, sliced into 1/16th-inch
 pieces
carrots, cut crosswise into rounds
celery, cut diagonally into 1-inch
 pieces
broccoli flowerets
green peppers, cut into strips
sliced mushrooms
pea pods
sliced waterchestnuts
bean sprouts

Heat small amount of chicken broth in wok or heavy skillet; add vegetables, beginning with those requiring the most cooking time. Stir-fry until all vegetables are just crisp-tender, add more broth as needed.

Note: If using a wok, pull vegetables up onto side of pan as they finish cooking.

Variation: Toss stir-fried vegetables with cooked Buckwheat (soba) noodles, asparagus, scallops or chicken.

SAUTÉED MUSHROOMS

3   tablespoons white wine or vermouth
1   clove garlic
1   pound fresh mushrooms, caps or
      pieces

Heat wine or vermouth and garlic in a heavy skillet. Add mushrooms. Cook uncovered over medium heat, stirring frequently 3-4 minutes.

Variations: Use 2 tablespoons wine or vermouth plus 1 tablespoon olive oil or safflower oil.

Use 3 tablespoons lemon juice; omit garlic.

SAUTÉED VEGETABLES

¼   cup white wine or vermouth
1   clove garlic
1   pound fresh mushrooms, caps or
      pieces
1   15-oz. can quartered artichoke
      hearts, drained
10 cherry tomatoes

Heat wine or vermouth and garlic in a heavy skillet; add mushrooms and artichokes. Cook uncovered over medium heat, stirring frequently 3-4 minutes. Add tomatoes; toss.

Variations: Use 2 tablespoons wine or vermouth plus 1 tablespoon olive oil or safflower oil.

Use ¼ cup lemon juice; omit the garlic.

Add chopped onion and chopped green pepper.

ONION RINGS

3 large white onions
1 cup flour
¼ teaspoon or less salt
¼ cup egg substitute
1 cup skim milk
1 tablespoon safflower oil

Cut onions into rings ½-inch thick. Mix flour and salt. Beat egg substitute; add milk and oil. Gradually add to flour; beat with wire whisk until smooth. Dip onion into batter; let drain on wire rack. Heat a small amount of safflower oil in a heavy skillet; cook onions 4-5 minutes. Turn; cook 2-3 minutes.

Variation: In place of onions substitute cauliflowerets, or eggplant cut into strips ½-inch thick and ½-inch long, or carrots cut crosswise into rounds.

ONIONS VINAIGRETTE

1 large white onion
dressing of oil and vinegar* (page 184)
basil
pepper

Slice onions into very thin rings. Drizzle with dressing of oil and vinegar. Sprinkle lightly with basil and freshly ground pepper.

BAKED ONIONS

½ cup safflower oil
3 tablespoons wine vinegar
¼ teaspoon basil
¼ teaspoon thyme
¼ teaspoon oregano
¼ teaspoon pepper
⅛ teaspoon salt
2 large onions, sliced into rings

Combine all ingredients, except onions, in a covered jar; shake. Pour over onions. Chill overnight, turning 2-3 times. Bake covered at 350° for 30 minutes. Uncover; bake 30 minutes longer or until onions are tender.

FRIED ONIONS

⅓ cup chicken broth* (page 149) or
   beef broth* (page 152)
2 medium onions, thinly sliced into
   rings
   ground pepper

Heat broth over high heat in wok or heavy skillet. Add onions; stir-fry until tender. Sprinkle with ground pepper.

COTTAGE FRIES

1   potato per person
½   teaspoon safflower oil per potato

Boil or steam potatoes in their jackets; peel. Slice thin. Toss with oil. Brown in a teflon skillet over medium heat, turning frequently.

Variation: For Potatoes O'Brien sauté chopped onion and chopped green pepper in a small amount of water or broth until tender. Toss with potatoes and oil. Brown.

FRENCH FRIED POTATOES

1   potato per person

Cut potatoes into strips. Arrange on a teflon baking sheet. Bake at 425° 15-20 minutes or until brown. Turn; bake 15-20 minutes or until tender.

Note: To shorten baking time, parboil potatoes 15 minutes; slice and roast.

Variation: Before cooking brush with safflower oil and sprinkle with garlic powder, onion powder, chili powder or celery seed.

HASH BROWN POTATOES

===

1   potato per person
¾   teaspoon onion per potato (optional)
½   teaspoon safflower oil per potato
    dash salt
    dash pepper

Boil or steam potatoes in their jackets. Chill. Peel. Shred. Toss with onion, oil, salt, and pepper. Pat into thin patties. Brown in a teflon skillet over medium heat 10-12 minutes. Turn. Brown 8-10 minutes longer or to desired brownness. For extra crispness, using two spatulas, cut horizontally through center of patty; flip one half over the other.

POTATO CHIPS

===

1   potato per person
    safflower oil

Slice potatoes crosswise into paper-thin rounds; brush with safflower oil. Bake on a teflon baking sheet at 425° 20 minutes. Turn; bake 15-20 minutes or until brown and crisp.

TWICE-BAKED POTATOES

4 potatoes
¼ cup hot skim milk
½ cup grated low-fat Cheddar cheese
paprika

Bake potatoes in their jackets (do not use new potatoes). Cut potatoes in half lengthwise; scoop out centers. Mash. Beat with hot milk. Mound back into skins. Sprinkle with cheese. Top with paprika. Bake at 400° for 20 minutes.

POTATOES WITH ONION AND DILL

1 pound small new potatoes, unpeeled
1 small red onion, thinly sliced
1 green pepper, thinly sliced into rings
1 cup plain low-fat yogurt* (page 114)
1 tablespoon chopped fresh dill or
   ¼ teaspoon dried dill
2 tablespoons safflower oil
2 tablespoons olive oil
¼ teaspoon or less salt
⅛ teaspoon pepper

Scrub potatoes; boil or steam until just tender. Place whole or sliced into a serving bowl; tuck onion and green pepper slices among potatoes. Combine yogurt, dill, oils, salt and pepper. Pass with potatoes.

LEMON POTATOES

1 pound small red potatoes
2 tablespoons beef broth* (page 152) or chicken broth* (page 149)
¼ cup fresh lemon juice
zest of ½ lemon
¼ teaspoon pepper
chopped chives
chopped fresh parsley
pinch rosemary

Slice potatoes into thin rounds; steam until just tender. Heat broth and lemon juice, but do not boil; pour over potatoes. Season with pepper. Sprinkle with chives, parsley and rosemary.

POTATOES EPICURE

3-4 medium potatoes
tub safflower mayonnaise
¾ cup cream of chicken soup* (page 158)
1 cup plain low-fat yogurt* (page 114)
¾ cup grated, low-fat Cheddar cheese
3 tablespoons chopped onion
1 tablespoon safflower oil
½ cup crushed corn flakes

Boil potatoes in their skins; cut into cubes. Grease an 8-inch square casserole with tub safflower margarine; add potatoes. Blend soup, yogurt, cheese and onions; pour over potatoes. Mix safflower oil with corn flakes; sprinkle over potatoes. Bake at 350° 30-40 minutes.

NEW POTATOES AND FRESH VEGETABLES

    1   pound new potatoes or small red
         potatoes
¼ - ½   lb. fresh green beans, steamed
    1   red or green pepper, cut into rings
    1   cucumber, sliced
    8   cherry tomatoes
    ½   pound fresh mushrooms
    1   cup plain low-fat yogurt* (page 114)
 1½   tablespoons Dijon mustard
    2   green onions, finely chopped
         dill weed to taste
         fresh parsley for garnish

Boil or steam potatoes with jackets until tender; cut into wedges. Chill potatoes and vegetables. Combine yogurt, mustard, green onion and dill to make dressing. Chill. Just before serving, arrange vegetables on a platter; place yogurt dressing in the center. Garnish with fresh parsley.

ALMOND PEAS

===

 1   lb. fresh green peas, washed, shelled
       and steamed
⅓   cup slivered almonds

Drain peas; toss with almonds.

FAT-FREE GRAVY

===

 2   cups chicken broth* (page 149) or
       beef broth* (page 152)
 3   tablespoons defatted meat juices (optional)
¼   cup flour
½   cup cold water
       salt to taste
       pepper to taste

Bring broth and defatted meat drippings to a boil.
Shake flour and water in a covered jar to form a
smooth paste; gradually add to boiling broth. Reduce heat; simmer 5-10 minutes, stirring constantly until thick. Season.

Note: To defat meat juices and drippings, pour the
juices and drippings into a bowl; add a few ice
cubes. Chill in the freezer 10-15 minutes or until
the fat congeals at the top and around ice cubes.
Discard ice cubes and congealed fat.

It is not necessary to use meat juices and drippings to make a satisfactory gravy with the above
recipe.

Variation: For a gravy that is especially good with
poultry, instead of 2 cups broth, use 1 cup milk and
1 cup broth.

MINTED PEAS

1   pound fresh green peas, washed,
        shelled and steamed
    fresh mint

Add fresh mint to peas while steaming.

CANNED TOMATOES

Thoroughly wash tomatoes. Put 4-5 at a time in boiling water, then dip in cold water. Peel. Cut out stem ends. Tightly pack tomatoes into clean, quart-size canning jars. Add 1½ teaspoons salt (or less) and ½ teaspoon citric acid to each jar. Adjust caps. Slowly lower jars into canner of boiling water. (Be sure there is enough water in the canner to cover tops of jars). When water again comes to a rolling boil, begin timing. Process 45 minutes, keeping water boiling vigorously entire time. Remove jars from canner. Cool upright on a thick cloth. After 24 hours test seal. Label jars. Store.

Note: If you have not canned before, consult a good canning cookbook before proceeding.

Helpful Hint: Many Positive Diet recipes use canned tomatoes. I try to can 2-3 flats of tomatoes each summer in order to have the sodium control that is not possible with commercially canned products.

BROILED TOMATO HALVES

ripe tomatoes
olive oil
ground pepper
fresh or dried basil
bread crumbs

Cut tomatoes into halves; brush lightly with olive oil. Sprinkle with pepper and basil. Top with bread crumbs. Broil 2-3 minutes.

VERA CRUZ TOMATOES

¼ cup chopped onion
  wine, broth or water
1 bunch fresh spinach, chopped
½ cup plain low-fat yogurt* (page 114)
  dash Tabasco sauce
4 medium tomatoes
½ cup grated Mozzarella cheese

Sauté onion in small amount of wine, broth or water until tender; add spinach and cook 3-4 minutes. Cool, drain and squeeze excess water from spinach. Mix spinach and onion with yogurt and Tabasco sauce. Cut tops from tomatoes and remove centers, leaving shells. Fill shells with spinach mixture. Place in a baking dish. Bake at 375° for 20-25 minutes. Top with cheese; bake 2-3 minutes longer or until cheese is melted.

HERBED TOMATOES

1 tomato per person
1 teaspoon red wine vinegar per
     tomato
   pinch chopped fresh parsley
   pinch thyme
   pinch basil
   pinch marjoram
   dash pepper

Slice tomatoes. Sprinkle with vinegar and herbs.

SESAME SPINACH

1 bunch fresh spinach
½ teaspoon sesame oil
4 teaspoons lemon juice
4 tablespoons toasted sesame seeds

Wash spinach in ice water; remove thick stems. Pat dry; tear into bite-size pieces. Toss with sesame oil; sprinkle with lemon juice and sesame seeds. Toss again.

ZUCCHINI AND CARROTS JULIENNE

---

1   medium zucchini
2-3   medium carrots
¼-½   cup chicken broth* (page 149) or
    beef broth* (page 152)
freshly ground pepper

Cut zucchini and carrots into julienne strips. Heat broth in wok or heavy skillet; add carrots; stir-fry 5-6 minutes. Add zucchini; stir-fry until carrots and zucchini are crisp-tender. Sprinkle with pepper.

CHEESE-STUFFED ZUCCHINI

---

3   small zucchini
¼   cup egg substitute, beaten
½   cup Ricotta cheese
½   cup low-fat Cheddar cheese
½   cup chopped fresh parsley
¼-½   cup bread crumbs

Slice zucchini lengthwise into halves. Steam until just barely tender; drain, pat dry and scoop out pulp. Combine egg, Ricotta cheese, Cheddar cheese, and parsley; fill zucchini shells. Sprinkle with bread crumbs. Arrange zucchini in baking dish greased with tub safflower margarine. Bake at 350° for 25 minutes. Place under broiler 2-3 minutes to brown bread crumbs.

ZUCCHINI-MOZZARELLA CASSEROLE

2   pounds zucchini (about 7 cups)
1   cup egg substitute, beaten
½   cup skim milk
¼   teaspoon or less salt
2   teaspoons baking powder
3   tablespoons flour
¼   cup chopped parsley
1   clove garlic, minced
1   small onion, finely chopped
1   7-oz. can diced green chilies
¾   pound Mozzarella cheese,
      grated
1   teaspoon herb seasoning* (page 115)
1   cup croutons
3   tablespoons safflower oil

Slice zucchini crosswise into ¼-inch thick slices. Whirl egg substitute, milk, salt, baking powder and flour in blender; add parsley, garlic and onion and whirl again. Pour into large mixing bowl; add zucchini, green chilies and cheese. Toss. Spoon into a greased 9x13x2-inch baking dish or 2 square 8-inch pans (the square ones are nice if you want to eat one and freeze the other). Sprinkle with herb seasoning. Toss croutons with safflower oil; sprinkle over top of casserole. Bake uncovered at 350° for 40 minutes or until zucchini is tender and mixture is set in the center. Let stand 10 minutes before serving.

PASTA PRIMAVERA WITH TOMATOES

1   lb. fresh tomatoes or one 1-lb. can
      plum tomatoes, puréed in blender
2   cloves garlic, minced
3   carrots, sliced into rounds
1   small bunch broccoli (flowerets only)
3   small zucchini, sliced into rounds
3   green onions, chopped
1   fresh tomato, chopped
1½ tablespoons safflower oil
1½ tablespoons olive oil
¼   teaspoon pepper
½   teaspoon dried basil or 2
      tablespoons fresh basil
¼   teaspoon or less salt
1   lb. wheel- or shell-shaped pasta cooked

Heat ¼ of the puréed tomatoes in wok or heavy skillet. Add garlic and carrots; stir-fry until carrots are crisp-tender. Add broccoli; stir-fry 2-3 minutes. Add zucchini and green onion; stir-fry 1-2 minutes. Add remaining ingredients; toss and heat. Serve over pasta.

PASTA PRIMAVERA WITH DIJON

1   lb. shell-shaped pasta, cooked
1   bunch green onions, chopped
2   large fresh tomatoes, diced
1   cup safflower oil
½   cup olive oil
½   cup cider vinegar
1   teaspoon Dijon mustard
    dash garlic powder
    salt and pepper to taste

Toss macaroni with green onions and tomatoes. Combine oils, vinegar and Dijon; pour enough over pasta to moisten. Season. Serve hot or cold.

PASTA WITH FRESH TOMATOES, BASIL AND CHEESE

7   ripe tomatoes, cut into ½"-chunks
1   cup fresh basil leaves, chopped
2   tablespoons chopped fresh parsley
3   large cloves garlic, minced
¾   teaspoon crushed red pepper
⅛   teaspoon salt (optional)
1   pound Mozzarella cheese,
    cubed
⅓   cup safflower oil
2   tablespoons olive oil
1   pound sea shell-shaped pasta

Combine tomatoes, basil, parsley, garlic, red pepper, salt, cheese, safflower oil and olive oil; let stand for 1 hour at room temperature. Cook pasta, drain; toss with tomatoes while still hot.

FETTUCCINI NAPOLI

1 pound fettuccini, cooked
1 cup olive oil
4 cloves garlic, minced
   juice of 1 lemon
¼ cup chopped fresh parsley
1 teaspoon fresh basil or ½ teaspoon
      dried basil
½ teaspoon oregano
½ teaspoon or less salt
¼ teaspoon pepper

Place fettuccini in large serving bowl. Combine remaining ingredients; pour over fettuccini. Toss.

FETTUCCINI WITH FRESH BASIL AND TOMATOES

2 lbs. ripe tomatoes, peeled and
      chopped
1 white onion, finely chopped
2 cloves garlic, chopped
¾ cup fresh basil, chopped
½ cup olive oil
   salt and pepper to taste
1 pound fettuccini, cooked
1 cup low-fat Cheddar cheese, grated

Mix tomatoes, onion, garlic, basil, olive oil, salt and pepper; let stand at room temperature for 1 hour. Cook fettuccini; drain. Toss with sauce; sprinkle with cheese. Serve at once.

MACARONI AND CHEESE

2   cups skim milk
3   tablespoons flour
½   teaspoon or less salt
    pinch pepper
¼   cup chopped onion
2   cups grated low-fat Cheddar cheese
3½ cups cooked macaroni
1-2 ripe tomatoes, sliced

Combine milk and flour in a covered jar; shake to form a smooth paste. Pour into a large saucepan; cook over medium heat, stirring constantly until thick. Add salt, pepper, onion and cheese. Stir until cheese is melted. Add macaroni. Toss. Pour into a 1½-quart casserole. Arrange tomato slices over top, pushing edge of each slice into macaroni. Bake uncovered at 350° for 45 minutes.

HUNGRY JOE SPECIAL

1   pound extra-lean ground round
1   onion, chopped
½   pound fresh mushrooms, sliced
1   bunch fresh spinach
    black pepper
1   cup egg substitute, beaten
½   cup Mozzarella or Cheddar
      cheese, grated

Brown beef; drain off excess fat. Add onions and mushrooms; simmer 10 minutes. Wash spinach; steam 3-4 minutes. Squeeze out excess moisture. Sprinkle with black pepper; toss with ground round. Scramble egg substitute in a teflon skillet; toss with ground round and spinach. Top with cheese. Toss again.

Accompany with sliced tomatoes.

DRIED BEANS, PEAS AND LENTILS

Soak beans using method 1 or method 2.

Soaking Method 1. Stir 1 teaspoon salt into 6 cups of water for each 1 pound of dried beans. Wash beans; add to salted water. Soak overnight. Drain. Rinse. Discard soaking water.

Soaking Method 2. Bring 8 cups of water for each 1 pound of beans to a boil. Wash beans, add to boiling water. Bring to a second boil; boil 2 minutes. Remove from heat; cover and let soak for 1 hour. Drain. Rinse. Discard soaking water.

Cook soaked beans as follows: For 1 pound of soaked beans bring 6 cups of water, chicken broth* (page 149) or beef broth* (page 152), 1 teaspoon salt and 1 onion to a boil. Add beans; boil gently, uncovered, 25 minutes to 2 hours or until tender. Cooking times will vary according to types used. Add more water or broth as necessary during cooking to keep beans covered.

One pound beans yields 6 cups cooked beans.

Note: Dry legumes are important sources of B vitamins, iron, calcium and potassium. They contain no cholesterol, are low in sodium and are good sources of fiber.

BAKED BEANS

3 cups small red beans or pinto beans, cooked
1 large onion, chopped
1 8-oz. can tomato sauce
⅓ cup molasses
1 teaspoon dry mustard
1 teaspoon chili powder

Combine beans, onion, tomato sauce, molasses, mustard, and chili powder; pour into a bean pot or casserole dish. Bake uncovered at 350° for 1 hour. Cover and continue baking for 30 minutes.

WILD RICE

1 small onion, chopped
2 cups beef broth* (page 152)
½ pound mushrooms, sliced
½ cup wild rice
1 cup brown long grain rice
2 tablespoons chopped fresh parsley

Sauté onion in small amount of broth until tender; add mushrooms and remaining broth. Bring to a boil; add wild rice and onion. Cover; reduce heat and simmer 20 minutes. Add long grain rice; return to boiling. Cover, reduce heat and simmer 20 minutes longer or until liquid is absorbed and rice is tender. Sprinkle with parsley.

TABBOULI PILAF

2	tablespoons safflower oil
1	medium onion, chopped
½	cup chopped celery
½	pound fresh mushrooms, sliced
1	cup uncooked bulgar wheat
¼	teaspoon oregano
¼	teaspoon salt
¼	teaspoon pepper
2	cups beef broth* (page 152)

Warm oil in heavy skillet over medium heat; add onions and celery. Cook 5 minutes. Add mushrooms and bulgar; cook, stirring constantly for 10 minutes or until bulgar is golden brown and vegetables are tender. Add oregano, salt, pepper and broth. Cover and bring to a boil; reduce heat and simmer 15-20 minutes or until broth is absorbed.

Variations: Use chicken broth* (page 149), rather than beef broth.

Sprinkle with chopped fresh parsley just before serving.

Add ¼ teaspoon dill weed to broth.

RICE PILAF

---

uncooked rice
chicken broth* (page 149)
finely chopped fresh parsley

Cook rice as directed on package, substituting chicken broth for the required water. Just before serving, toss rice with parsley. Spoon into ring mold; pat down. Unmold.

BREAD STUFFING

1	large onion, chopped
3	stalks celery, chopped
2½	cups chicken broth* (page 149)
½	pound fresh mushrooms, sliced
10–12	cups dried bread crumbs
2	tablespoons safflower oil
1¼	teaspoon sage
½	teaspoon or less salt
¼	teaspoon pepper

Sauté onion and celery in small amount of broth until tender. Add mushrooms; cook 2-3 minutes. Add bread cubes. Toss with oil. Gradually moisten with broth, adding a little more or a little less broth as necessary. Season. Toss. Bake covered at 350° 30-40 minutes or until piping hot. Makes enough dressing to accompany a 10-14 pound turkey.

Note: On the Positive Diet, dressing should not be put into the turkey because as the turkey cooks, the fat in the bird drips into the dressing.

BARLEY AND MUSHROOM PILAF

1¾   cups pearl barley
1   onion, chopped
3   tablespoons safflower oil
½   pound fresh mushrooms, sliced
4   cups beef broth* (page 152)

Soak barley several hours or overnight in enough cold water to cover. Drain. Sauté onion and barley in safflower oil until onion is tender and barley is toasted, add mushrooms; cook 2-3 minutes longer. Spoon into large casserole. Heat broth to boiling; pour over barley. Stir. Bake covered at 350° for 1 hour. Uncover; bake 1 to 1½ hours longer or until liquid is absorbed.

CHAPTER SIXTEEN

SEAFOOD

Seafood

MARINATED FISH

1   pound fillet of halibut, swordfish,
       red snapper or other white
       fish
3   tablespoons safflower oil
2   tablespoons olive oil
2   cloves garlic, minced
    pinch paprika

Marinate fish in safflower oil, olive oil and garlic
for 1 hour; drain. Sprinkle with paprika. Broil 5-10
minutes or until fish flakes, turning only once; do
not overcook.

Variation: Serve with herbed mayonnaise* (page
182) or Dijon vinaigrette* (page 183).

Helpful Hint: Correct Timing for Fish: measure the fish
at the thickest point and allow 10 minutes cooking
time per inch. If a salmon measures 3-inches at its
thickest point, the total cooking time would be 30
minutes (10x3); 15 minutes per side. A halibut roast
that is 1-inch thick would require 10 minutes total
cooking time; 5 minutes per side. Always test fish a
few minutes early, just to be on the safe side.

Testing For Doneness: Fish is done the second it
loses translucency and flakes easily when probed
with a fork at its thickest point. When testing a
whole fish, probe an inch or two below the base of
the head, and again at the thickest point behind
the abdominal cavity. When fish is opaque and
milky and detaches easily from the bone, it is
done.

STUFFED WHOLE FISH

¾   cup safflower oil
¼   cup olive oil
1   whole salmon, trout, cod or other
     whole fish
     sage to taste
     pepper to taste
1   onion, sliced into rings
2-3   stalks celery, cut into 3-inch lengths
¼   pound fresh mushrooms, sliced
2-3   carrots, peeled, quartered and cut into
     2-inch lengths
2   fresh lemons, sliced into rounds

Pour safflower oil and olive oil over fish; add more if necessary to generously cover fish inside and outside. Marinate 1-4 hours.

Remove fish from oil and season with sage and black pepper. Stuff inside cavity to bulging with onions, celery, mushrooms and carrots.

Place fish on aluminum foil; slide a layer of lemon rounds under fish. Place more lemon slices on top of fish; fish should be smothered top and bottom with lemon rounds. Wrap fish in two thicknesses of foil. Bake at 425° or grill over deep coals until fish flakes

CRAB STUFFED TROUT

- 3 tablespoons safflower oil
- 1 tablespoon olive oil
- 2-3 6-8 oz. trout, heads and tails removed
- 1 small onion, thinly sliced
- ¼ pound crab meat
- ¼ pound fresh mushrooms, sliced
  juice of ½ lemon
- 3 tablespoons dry vermouth
  fresh lemon wedges
  fresh parsley

Place fish in 9x13x2-inch baking dish. Pour safflower oil and olive oil over fish, add more if necessary to generously cover fish inside and outside. Marinate 10 minutes. Pour off oil; stuff inside cavity with onion, crab and mushrooms.

Combine lemon juice and vermouth; pour over fish both inside and outside. Cover baking dish with aluminum foil.

Bake at 400° about 20 minutes or until skin pulls easily away from fish. Baste frequently during cooking. Serve with plenty of fresh lemon; garnish with parsley.

Note: For a refreshing dessert, try Lemon Ice* (page 290).

Variation: Any other type of whole fish may be used in place of trout.

COURT BOUILLON

2   quarts cold water
1   quart dry white wine
¾   cup wine vinegar
2   carrots, cut into 1-inch pieces
2   stalks celery with leaves, cut into
     2-inch pieces
2   onions, thinly sliced
4   sprigs parsley
1   lemon, thinly sliced
1   bay leaf
1   teaspoon thyme
2-3 peppercorns

Prepare as for easy court bouillon.

EASY COURT BOUILLON

2   quarts chicken broth* (page 149)
1   quart dry white wine
2   onions, minced
3   sprigs parsley
¼   cup safflower oil
¼   cup olive oil
    pinch crushed thyme

Combine all ingredients for court bouillon or for easy court bouillon in a stock pot; bring to a boil. Reduce heat; simmer uncovered 45 minutes.

Note: With the exception of bouillon that has been used to poach salmon, court bouillon and easy court bouillon may be used several times over and they may also be frozen.

230

POACHED FISH

1   3-6 pound whole fish fillet, head and
      tail removed, if desired
2   tablespoons lemon juice
2   quarts cold water
1   recipe court bouillon* or easy court
      bouillon* (page 232)

Clean and scale fish. Rinse in lemon juice and
water. Wrap in cheese cloth; twist ends and tie
with string. Place in fish poacher or roasting pan
over 2 burners; cover with court bouillon or easy
court bouillon and bring to a boil.

Reduce heat to simmer and begin timing; allow
10 minutes of cooking time per inch of thickness,
20 minutes if frozen. Be careful not to overcook;
remember the fish will continue to cook even
when removed from heat. Serve hot or cold.

BROILED FILLETS WITH FRESH LEMON

1   pound fillet of halibut, red snapper,
      cod, sole or other white fish
    juice of 1 lemon
    grated rind of 1 lemon
    lemon slices for garnish
    watercress for garnish
    salt and pepper to taste

Marinate fish in lemon juice and lemon rind at
least 2 hours and all day, if possible, turning
frequently. Broil 10-15 minutes, turning only once.
Serve over lemon slices. Garnish with watercress.
Season to taste.

BAKED FILLETS WITH LEMON AND FENNEL

1   pound fillet of halibut, red snapper,
     cod, sole or other white fish
2   tablespoons safflower oil
     juice of 1 lemon
2-3   green onions, finely chopped
1   bunch fresh fennel or 2 teaspoons
     dried fennel

Brush fish with safflower oil; cover with lemon juice. Sprinkle with green onion and fennel (if fresh fennel is available, slice fennel lengthwise and place fish on top). Bake at 375° 10-20 minutes or until fish flakes.

Variation: Serve with homemade safflower mayonnaise* (page 182).

FILLETS WITH VERMOUTH AND ORANGE SAUCE

1 pound fillet of halibut, red snapper, cod, sole or other white fish
3 tablespoons safflower oil
1 tablespoon olive oil
½ cup fresh orange juice
½ cup dry vermouth
1 orange, thinly sliced for garnish
    watercress for garnish

Marinate fish for 1 hour in safflower and olive oil. Heat orange juice and vermouth just to boiling; reduce heat and simmer 2-3 minutes. Pour over fish. Bake at 450° 15-20 minutes, basting frequently. When fish is done, pour juices into a saucepan; boil 3-4 minutes to reduce. Spread a serving plate with orange slices; top with fish. Cover with sauce. Garnish with watercress.

FILLETS WITH FRESH VEGETABLES AND CHEESE

¼	pound fresh mushrooms, sliced water, wine or broth
1-2	green onions, finely chopped
1	tomato, diced
¼	teaspoon basil
¼	teaspoon lemon pepper or black pepper
1	egg beaten or ¼ cup egg substitute, beaten
¾	cup grated low-fat Cheddar cheese
1	pound fillet of halibut, red snapper, sole, cod or other white fish
1	teaspoon safflower oil

Steam mushrooms in small amount of water, wine or broth for 2-3 minutes. Toss with green onions, tomato, basil, pepper, egg and cheese; brush fish with safflower oil. Bake at 500° 5-8 minutes or until fish is just barely tender. Cover with vegetables and cheese. Broil 5 minutes or until cheese melts.

FILLETS WITH WINE AND TOMATO SAUCE

1 onion, chopped
2-3 stalks celery, chopped
2 carrots, diced
1 clove garlic, minced
1 cup white wine
2 tablespoons safflower oil
1 8-oz. can tomato sauce
3 tablespoons chopped parsley
1 pound fillet of halibut, red snapper,
sole, cod or other white fish

Sauté vegetables in small amount of wine until tender; add oil, tomato sauce, parsley and remaining wine. Simmer 15 minutes. Pour ¼ of the sauce into a baking dish; arrange fish on top. Cover with remaining sauce. Bake covered at 350° 15-20 minutes.

FRESH SOLE WITH YOGURT AND CHEESE

fresh sole fillets
fresh lemon juice
grated onion
plain low-fat yogurt* (page 114)
Tabasco sauce
Mozzarella cheese, grated

Arrange sole in a baking dish; drizzle with lemon juice. Top with grated onion; spread with yogurt. Drizzle with Tabasco sauce. Bake at 350° for 10 minutes; top with cheese. Bake 10 minutes longer or until fish flakes and cheese has melted.

FISH ORIENTAL STYLE

1 pound fillet of sole, cod, turbot,
     halibut or other white fish
6 tablespoons sake
3 tablespoons ginger juice
3 tablespoons lemon juice
     pinch salt
6 Shitake mushrooms
1-2 fresh lemons, cut into wedges

Place each fillet on a piece of aluminum foil; fold edges of foil upwards to make a bowl. Cover each fillet with generous amount of sake, ginger juice and lemon juice; top with 1-2 mushrooms. Pinch top edges of foil together to seal, leaving a small amount of space between top of fish and top of foil. Steam in a 350° oven for 20 minutes or until done. Garnish with plenty of fresh lemon.

Note: Shitake mushrooms can usually be found in oriental markets. If fresh are unavailable, reconstitute dried Shitake mushrooms by soaking them in water for 30 minutes or until soft.

LINGUINE WITH TUNA SAUCE

---

3   large ripe tomatoes, chopped
2   tablespoons olive oil
½   cup chopped fresh parsley
1   bunch green onions with tops,
     chopped
½   teaspoon chopped fresh basil or
     ¼ teaspoon dried basil
1   lemon
1   6½-oz. can water pack tuna, drained
1   teaspoon pepper
¾   pound linguine, cooked

Combine tomatoes, oil, parsley, green onion and basil; cook 5-7 minutes. Squeeze lemon over tuna. Grate rind of lemon; sprinkle over tuna and toss with pepper. Add to tomatoes and onion; cook 5-7 minutes. Serve over linguine.

TUNA NOODLE CASSEROLE

---

1   8-oz. package macaroni,
     cooked
1   6½-oz. can water pack tuna, drained
1   8-oz. can sliced waterchestnuts,
     drained
3   cups cream of chicken soup*
     (page 158)

Combine all ingredients. Pour into a 2-quart casserole. Bake at 375° for 25-30 minutes.

CHAPTER SEVENTEEN

POULTRY

ROAST TURKEY

1   turkey
    sage
    pepper
    garlic powder
2-3   stalks celery, cut into 2-inch pieces
1-2   onions, quartered

Wipe inside of turkey with a damp paper towel; wash outside with cold water. Rub inside cavity with sage, pepper and garlic powder. Place celery and onions inside cavity. Skewer neck skin to back; tuck wing tips behind shoulder joints.

Place breast side up on rack in shallow roasting pan; roast at 325°. Turkey is done when drum sticks move easily or twist out of joint. A meat thermometer should register 195°. If turkey browns too quickly, cover it with a cap of aluminum foil.

Roasting Chart
  6-8   pounds 2¾ to 3½ hours
  8-12 pounds 3¼ to 4   hours
12-16 pounds 3¾ to 5   hours
16-20 pounds 4¾ to 6½ hours
20-24 pounds 6¼ to 8   hours

Note: For Positive Diet purposes the turkey should not be stuffed as fat from the turkey drips into the dressing. There is an excellent stuffing recipe in this book that is cooked along side the turkey.

Helpful Hint: Be sure to save the carcass for soup.

ROAST TURKEY BREAST

turkey breasts
safflower oil
sage

Remove skin from breast; rub with safflower oil and season with sage. Roast on a rack at 350° for 1½-hours or until juices run free when pricked with a fork.

STEAMED TURKEY BREAST

turkey breast
lemon juice

Remove skin from turkey breast. Place breast in a steamer over boiling water and add a dash of lemon juice. Cover. Steam 30-35 minutes or until juices run free when pricked with a fork.

OVEN-FRIED CHICKEN

½-1   chicken breast per person
safflower oil
flour or bread crumbs
pinch pepper
paprika

Remove skin from chicken. Brush each piece with safflower oil. Dredge lightly in flour or bread crumbs. Season with pepper. Sprinkle with paprika. Bake at 425° 35-40 minutes. Turn; bake 10-25 minutes longer or until tender.

BAKED CHICKEN WITH OLIVE OIL AND FRESH LEMON

2 chicken breasts, halved
2 tablespoons safflower oil
2 tablespoons olive oil
¼ cup fresh lemon juice
1 clove garlic, minced
¼ teaspoon oregano
¼ teaspoon tarragon

Remove skin from chicken breasts; debone. Combine safflower oil, olive oil, lemon juice, garlic, oregano and tarragon; pour over chicken. Marinate 20 minutes. Bake at 350° 35-45 minutes or until done. Baste frequently during baking.

Helpful Hint: To debone chicken breasts, tear off skin. Break breast in two by splitting bone in center of breast. Cut meat free from the long rib cage bone. Then cut around upper edge of breast. Pull the rest of the meat away from bones. Loosen the tendons and remove.

To save chicken bones for soup, keep a plastic bag in the freezer just for bones reserved from boning breasts. When bag is full, add extra backs, necks and wings and make chicken soup.

MICROWAVE BAKED CHICKEN

2   chicken breasts, halved
    safflower oil

Remove skin from chicken breasts; debone. Brush with safflower oil. Place in glass pie plate — place larger pieces to the outside of dish. Cover with plastic wrap; prick for steam to escape. Cook 8 minutes; turn. Rearrange pieces in dish; cook 6 minutes longer or until done.

ROAST CHICKEN

1   3-4 pound chicken fryer chicken
    sage
    pepper
    garlic powder
2   stalks chopped celery with leaves
1   onion, quartered

Wipe inside of chicken with a damp paper towel; wash outside with cold water. Rub inside cavity with sage, pepper and garlic powder. Place celery and onions inside cavity. Skewer neck skin to back; tuck wing tips behind shoulder joints. Place breast side up in shallow roasting pan. Roast 60-75 minutes at 350°. Let stand 10 minutes before slicing.

Serve with oven-roasted vegetables.

Note: Be sure to save the carcass for soup.

ROAST CHICKEN ORIENTAL STYLE

1   bunch leaf lettuce
1   roast chicken, thinly sliced* (page 246)
1   bunch green onions with tops
12   spring roll (lumpia) wrappers
     hot Chinese mustard
     toasted sesame seeds

Tear lettuce into bite-size pieces; arrange on a platter or tray. Layer chicken over lettuce. Slice green onions lengthwise into 2-inch strips; arrange around edge of lettuce.

Place spring roll wrappers in a vegetable steamer rack over boiling water; steam 3-5 minutes or until hot or wrap spring roll wrappers in a damp tea towel and steam 1-2 minutes in the microwave. Remove to a napkin-lined basket.

Everyone prepares their own meal as follows: Lay spring roll wrapper flat. Place a slice of chicken, some lettuce and green onion lengthwise in center of wrapper. Fold bottom edge up, left and right sides over and roll as for crêpes.

POACHED CHICKEN

tub safflower margarine
4 chicken breasts
½ fresh lemon
¼ cup dry white wine
¼ cup chicken broth* (page 149)
pinch pepper
pinch salt

Grease a baking dish with tub safflower margarine. Remove skin from chicken breast; debone. Arrange chicken breasts in baking dish; drizzle with lemon juice. Season. Add wine and broth. Cover dish tightly. Bake at 400° 10-15 minutes or until tender and no sign of pink remains.

STEAMED CHICKEN

chicken breasts
fresh lemon juice

Remove skin from chicken breast; debone if desired. Place breast in a vegetable steamer basket over boiling water; add a dash of lemon juice. Cover. Steam 15-25 minutes or until chicken is tender and no sign of pink remains; do not overcook.

Serve with fresh lemon wedges; sprinkle with ground pepper.

BARBECUED CHICKEN WITH SKEWERED VEGETABLES

3	chicken breasts
3	tablespoons safflower oil
1	tablespoon olive oil
¼	cup fresh lemon juice
1	teaspoon honey
	pinch tarragon
	pinch oregano
12	cherry tomatoes
12	fresh mushrooms
2	onions, cut into 2-inch cubes
2	green peppers, quartered
½	fresh pineapple, cut into chunks

Skin and debone chicken; cut into 2-inch cubes. Combine safflower oil, olive oil, lemon juice, honey and seasonings; pour over chicken and vegetables. Marinate 30-60 minutes.

Alternate chicken, vegetables and fruit on skewers. Broil 4-6 inches from heat, turning frequently and basting often about 20-30 minutes or until chicken is done.

Variation: Instead of chicken parts, roast a whole chicken. Skewer vegetables separately.

DIJON CHICKEN

1   chicken breast per person
1   recipe Dijon vinaigrette* (page 183)

Broil, grill, bake, steam, roast or poach chicken.
Accompany with Dijon vinaigrette for dipping.

CHICKEN-STUFFED PEPPERS

4   medium green peppers
⅓   cup chopped onion
1   1-lb. can stewed tomatoes
2   cups cooked barley or rice
¼   teaspoon Tabasco sauce
     pinch pepper
3   cooked chicken breasts, deboned
     and cubed
¾   cup grated Mozzarella or Cheddar
     cheese

Cut tops of green peppers; remove seeds and
membrane. Sauté onion in small amount of tomato
liquid; add tomatoes, rice or barley, Tabasco, pepper, chicken and ½ of the cheese. Stand peppers
upright in an 8-inch square baking dish; stuff
with tomato-barley filling. Bake uncovered at 350°
25-30 minutes or until hot; sprinkle with remaining cheese. Return to oven until cheese melts.

Variation: In place of chicken, use ¾-lb. extra lean
mince, cooked and drained.

STIR-FRIED CHICKEN WITH VEGETABLES

1   tablespoon ginger juice
1   tablespoon sake
1   pound deboned chicken breasts, cut
     into bite-sized pieces
2   tablespoons potato starch
1   cup chicken broth* (page 149)
1   onion, sliced into 1/16ths
¼   pound bamboo shoots, cut into
     2-inch lengths
3   stalks celery, sliced
1   carrot, sliced crosswise into rounds
2   green peppers, cut into 1/16ths
½   pound fresh snow peas
1   8-oz. can sliced waterchestnuts
½   pound fresh mushrooms, sliced

Grate ginger; squeeze pulp to get 1 tablespoon juice. Mix ginger juice with sake; pour over chicken. Let stand 10 minutes; sprinkle with potato starch.

Cook chicken in a pre-heated teflon skillet over medium-high heat until chicken turns white. Set aside.

Heat ½ cup of broth in wok or heavy skillet; stir-fry onions, bamboo shoots, celery and carrots until just crisp-tender. Stir in green pepper and snow peas; stir-fry 2-3 minutes. Add waterchestnuts and mushrooms; stir-fry 1-2 minutes. Add more broth as needed during cooking. Toss chicken with vegetables. Serve at once.

Note: Good with steamed rice.

STIR-FRIED CHICKEN WITH GREEN PEPPERS

1   pound deboned chicken breasts
1   tablespoon sake
2   tablespoons potato starch
½   cup chicken broth* (page 149)
4   green peppers, seeded and cut
      lengthwise into thin strips

Cut chicken into bite-size pieces; toss with sake. Let stand 10 minutes; sprinkle with potato starch. Cook in a pre-heated teflon skillet over medium high heat until chicken turns white. Set aside. Heat chicken broth in wok or heavy skillet; stir-fry green peppers 2-3 minutes or until just crisp-tender. Toss with chicken.

CHICKEN A LA KING

½   pound fresh mushrooms, sliced
½   green pepper, sliced
1½   cups cooked chicken, diced
1   recipe cream of chicken soup*
      (page 158)
      rice, or toast

Sauté mushrooms and green pepper in small amount of chicken broth, water or white wine until tender. Stir in chicken and soup. Heat to serving temperature. Serve over rice or toast.

Note: If serving over rice, pack rice into a ring mold. Turn out at once onto a hot platter. Fill center with chicken a la king.

CHICKEN CURRY

½ cup chopped onion
2 cups chicken broth* (page 149)
2 cups skim milk
½ cup flour
½ teaspoon or less salt
1 tablespoon curry powder
¼ teaspoon ground ginger
1 tablespoon lemon juice
4 cups cooked chicken, diced
1 8-oz. can sliced waterchestnuts
   steamed rice
   unsalted peanuts for garnish
      (optional)
   raisins for garnish (optional)
   pineapple chunks for garnish
      (optional)
   homemade chutney (optional)

Sauté onion in small amount of chicken broth until tender; add remaining broth. Bring to a boil. Shake milk and flour in a covered jar to form a smooth paste; gradually add to boiling broth, stirring constantly until thick. Add seasonings. Pour lemon juice over chicken; add to sauce. Stir in waterchestnuts. Heat. Serve over steamed rice. If desired, garnish with unsalted peanuts, raisins, pineapple chunks and chutney.

CHICKEN AND DUMPLINGS

1 3-pound chicken
1 onion, sliced
2 stalks celery, chopped
½ teaspoon or less salt
5 peppercorns
1 bay leaf
5 cups water
2 carrots, quartered lengthwise
½ pound fresh mushrooms, sliced
2 tablespoons flour plus ¼ cup water
¾ cup snow peas

Place chicken, onion, celery, salt, peppercorns, bay leaf and water in stock pot; heat to boiling. Cover, reduce heat and simmer 2-3 hours. Strain. Slice and wrap chicken. Refrigerate chicken and broth overnight. Skim fat. Shortly before serving, heat broth to boiling; add carrots and cook 10-15 minutes or until tender. Prepare dumplings.

Dumplings
1 cup flour
2 teaspoons baking powder
¼ teaspoon or less salt
½ cup skim milk
2 tablespoons safflower oil

Sift together flour, baking powder and salt. Combine milk and safflower oil and add to dry ingredients; stir just until moistened.
Continued

Add chicken and mushrooms to boiling broth; bring to a second boil. Drop dumplings by table-spoonsful on top of bubbling stew. Cover tightly; bring to a boil. Reduce heat; simmer 12-15 minutes. Caution: do not lift cover from dumplings during cooking process.

Remove dumplings from pan. Combine flour and water to make a smooth paste; quickly stir into broth to make a gravy. Add snow peas. Heat. Serve.

CHICKEN POT PIE

½ cup diced carrots
¼ cup diced celery
¼ cup chopped white onion
chicken broth* (page 149)
1½ cups cooked chicken, diced
3 cups cream of chicken soup* (page 158)
½ cup fresh snow peas
½ cup thinly sliced fresh mushrooms
⅛ teaspoon pepper
1 recipe double pie crust* (page 284)

Sauté carrots, celery and onion in small amount of chicken broth, water or white wine until tender. Add chicken, soup, remaining vegetables and seasoning; set aside. Roll out pastry dough. Line one 9-inch pie pan or 3-4 individual size pans with ½ of the dough. Fill with chicken filling. Adjust top crust. Tuck edges under and flute. Cut steam holes. Bake at 400° for 20 minutes or until lightly browned and inside mixture is bubbly.

CHICKEN CREOLE

1 medium onion, chopped
1 clove garlic, minced
½ cup celery, finely chopped
1 8-oz. can tomato sauce
½ cup water
1 bay leaf
¼ teaspoon salt
⅛ teaspoon cayenne
2 tablespoons safflower oil
1 green pepper, finely chopped
1 cup cooked chicken, cubed
1 teaspoon fresh parsley, chopped
steamed rice

Combine onion, garlic, celery, tomato sauce, water, bay leaf, salt, cayenne and safflower oil in a 4-quart saucepan; bring to a boil. Cover, reduce heat and simmer 45-60 minutes. Add green pepper and chicken. Cover; simmer 10-15 minutes. Sprinkle with parsley. Serve over steamed rice.

CHICKEN CACCIATORE

1 28-oz. can plum tomatoes
1 tablespoon safflower oil
1 onion, chopped
3 carrots, peeled and thinly sliced
3 stalks celery, thinly sliced
2 tablespoons red wine vinegar
¼ teaspoon pepper
¾ teaspoon sage
½ teaspoon or less salt
2 chicken breasts, halved
¾ pound shell-shaped pasta

Combine all ingredients, except chicken and pasta in a stew pot or Dutch oven; bring to a boil. Reduce heat; cover and simmer 25-30 minutes. Skin and debone chicken; add to sauce and cook 25-30 minutes or until tender. Serve over cooked pasta.

Note: Crusty French bread and a tossed green salad with oil and vinegar dressing are nice accompaniments.

CHILI CON POLLO

1	28-oz. can plum tomatoes
½	teaspoon or less salt
1½	teaspoons dry mustard
1½	teaspoons chili powder
2	small cloves garlic, minced
1	pound deboned, cooked chicken breast, diced
4	cups cooked red kidney beans
2	cups cooked macaroni

Combine tomatoes, salt, dry mustard, chili powder and garlic; simmer uncovered for 1½-2 hours. Add chicken and kidney beans; heat to boiling. Stir in pasta. Heat to serving temperature.

Variation: Two 15-oz. cans kidney beans with liquid may be used in place of the fresh.

CHICKEN TOSTADOS

corn tortillas
cooked chicken, cubed
lettuce, diced
ripe tomatoes, diced
white onion, diced
chopped green chilies (optional)
low-fat Cheddar or Mozzarella cheese,
   grated
tomato salsa* (page 183)
plain low-fat yogurt (optional)
   (page 114)

Place tortillas on a teflon baking sheet. Heat in a 350° oven 3 minutes; turn. Heat 3 more minutes or until warm. Spread tortillas with chicken; top with lettuce, tomato, onion, green chilies, cheese, salsa and yogurt.

Variation: Substitute extra-lean ground round for chicken.

CHICKEN ENCHILADAS

2   cups cooked chicken, shredded
1   small ripe tomato, chopped
1   onion, chopped
1   8-oz. can chopped green chilies
1¼ cups grated low-fat Cheddar cheese
1   recipe tomato salsa* (page 183)
8   corn tortillas
1   8-oz. can tomato puree
3   cloves garlic
3   drops Tabasco sauce

Combine chicken, tomato, ¼ cup chopped onion, 1 tablespoon chopped green chilies, 1 tablespoon cheese and 1 tablespoon salsa. Set aside. Heat tortillas on a teflon baking sheet in a 350° oven about 3 minutes on each side to soften. Put 3 tablespoons chicken filling in center of each tortilla and roll; arrange seam side down in a shallow oven-proof baking dish. Set aside. Place tomato puree, garlic and remaining onion in blender; purée until smooth. Stir in remaining green chilies and Tabasco sauce; pour over enchiladas. Bake at 375° 15 minutes. Sprinkle with remaining cheese. Bake 10 minutes longer.

LEMON CHICKEN WITH FRESH SPINACH

3 chicken breasts
1 tablespoon ginger juice
1 tablespoon sake
½ cup fresh lemon juice
2 cups chicken broth* (page 149)
¼ cup flour
½ cup water
2 tablespoons potato starch
1 bunch fresh spinach

Remove skin from chicken; debone and cut into cubes. Sprinkle with ginger juice and sake. Let stand 10 minutes.

Combine lemon juice and broth in medium saucepan; reserve ⅓ cup and set aside. Heat remainder to boiling. Shake flour and water in a covered jar to form a smooth paste; gradually add to boiling broth, stirring constantly until thick. Reduce heat and let simmer 5-10 minutes.

Sprinkle chicken with potato starch. Heat reserved broth in wok or heavy skillet; stir-fry chicken. Tear spinach into bite-size pieces; toss with chicken. Serve onto plates. Pour sauce over.

LEMON CHICKEN WITH MAYONNAISE AND FRESH TOMATOES

3   chicken breasts, halved
⅛   teaspoon safflower oil
¼   cup dry vermouth
¼   teaspoon white pepper
½   cup lemon juice
½   cup safflower mayonnaise
1   teaspoon grated onion
    watercress
    fresh tomato slices
    fresh parsley

Remove skin from chicken; debone. Brush with safflower oil. Lightly brown chicken on both sides in a teflon skillet; remove to baking dish.

Pour vermouth into skillet; bring to a boil and reduce by ⅓. Remove from heat; add white pepper and 6 tablespoons of the lemon juice; pour over chicken. Bake covered in a 350° oven for 20 minutes or until chicken is done. Baste frequently during cooking. Cool to room temperature. Refrigerate several hours.

Mix remaining lemon juice with mayonnaise and grated onion. Let chicken come to room temperature (about 1 hour) before serving; place on a bed of watercress that has been topped with sliced tomatoes. Garnish with parsley. Serve with lemon mayonnaise.

Note: Homemade safflower mayonnaise* (page 182) is especially good with this.

CHAPTER EIGHTEEN

RED MEATS

LAMB BURGERS

---

1   pound extra lean ground lamb
    pita bread
½   pound Mozzarella cheese, sliced
    red lettuce leaves
    sliced tomato
    sliced white onion

Press ground lamb into patties. Grill over hot coals or broil on rack 3-inches from heat, 4-6 minutes on each side. Turn when juices begin to form on top of meat. Serve into pita bread. Top with cheese, lettuce, tomato and onion.

SWISS STEAK

---

1   pound extra-lean flank
¼   cup flour
    pinch pepper
1   onion, cut into rings
¼   cup red wine
1   1-lb. can plum tomatoes

Shake meat in paper bag with flour and pepper. Brown onion and meat on both sides in wine. Drain, if necessary to remove any excess fat. Stir in tomatoes. Cover tightly. Cook slowly 1½-2 hours or until tender.

HAMBURGERS

extra lean ground round
French rolls, French bread or
   hamburger buns
tomato slices
lettuce
white onion slices
safflower mayonnaise

Press ground round into patties. Grill or broil on rack 3-inches from heat 4-6 minutes on each side. Turn when juices begin to form on top of meat. Serve immediately on warm buns, French bread or French rolls. Garnish with tomato slices, lettuce and onion.

TOSTADOS

8   corn tortillas
1   pound extra-lean ground round, cooked and drained
½   head of lettuce, chopped
2   ripe tomatoes, chopped
1   white onion, chopped
1   cup Mozzarella or Cheddar cheese, grated
1   recipe tomato salsa* (page 183)

Place tortillas on a teflon baking sheet. Heat in a 350° oven 3 minutes on each side or until warm. Spread with ground round. Top with lettuce, tomato, onion, cheese and salsa. Serve.

COUNTRY POT ROAST

2-3	pound chuck, blade, rump or pot roast
1	2-pound can plum tomatoes
2	teaspoons caraway seeds
½	teaspoon or less salt
2-3	drops Tabasco sauce (optional)
1	bay leaf
¼	teaspoon black pepper
4	potatoes, peeled and quartered
6	carrots, peeled and quartered
6	stalks celery, peeled and quartered
4	small onions
12	fresh mushrooms

Brown meat in a small amount of tomato liquid; drain, if necessary to remove any excess fat. Add tomatoes and seasonings. Cover and simmer 1½ hours; add potatoes, carrots, celery and onions. Cover and simmer about 1 hour — until vegetables are crisp-tender. Add mushrooms and simmer 15 minutes.

BEEF STEW

2	pounds chuck roast
1	2-pound can plum tomatoes
¼	teaspoon black pepper
¼	cup red wine (optional)
4	stalks celery, sliced on the diagonal into quarters
1	onion, cut into eighths
5	carrots, peeled and quartered
½	pound fresh mushrooms, sliced
½	pound fresh green beans, cooked
1	15-oz. can artichoke hearts
½	teaspoon safflower oil
3-4	drops hot chili oil (La Yu)
2	cups cooked macaroni

Brown chuck roast in small amount of tomato liquid; drain if necessary, to remove any excess fat. Add tomatoes, pepper and wine; bring to a boil. Add celery, onion and carrots; simmer 45 minutes. Add mushrooms, beans and artichoke hearts; simmer 15 minutes. Add safflower oil, chili oil and pasta. Heat.

Note: Hot chili oil (La Yu) is available in oriental markets.

OLD FASHIONED HASH

1½ cups coarsely ground left over roast
     or steak
3   coarsely ground cooked potatoes
½   onion, coarsely ground
¼   pound fresh mushrooms, coarsely
     ground
1   green pepper, coarsely ground
¼   cup chopped fresh parsley
½   teaspoon or less salt
¼ - ½ teaspoon black pepper
⅔   cup evaporated milk
⅓   cup crushed corn flakes plus
     1 tablespoon olive oil for
     topping (optional)

Combine all ingredients except corn flakes and olive oil. Grease a loaf pan with tub safflower margarine. Mold hash into pan. Sprinkle with corn flake topping, if desired. Bake at 350° 30 minutes or until hot. Serve with ketchup and mustard.

DUTCH MEAT LOAF

- 1 15-oz. can tomato sauce
- ¼ cup water
- 2 tablespoons prepared mustard
- 1 tablespoon vinegar
- 1 pound extra-lean ground round
- 1 cup bread crumbs
- ¼ cup egg substitute
- 1 medium onion, chopped
- ¼ teaspoon pepper

Combine tomato sauce, water, mustard and vinegar. Mix beef with bread crumbs, egg, onion, pepper and ¼ of the tomato sauce mixture. Shape into a loaf pan. Pour enough sauce over top of meat loaf to coat. Bake at 350° for 1 hour, basting often. Warm remaining sauce; serve over sliced meat loaf.

OVEN TACOS

4   corn tortillas
1   pound extra-lean ground round,
        cooked and drained
1   cup grated low-fat Cheddar cheese
1   white onion, chopped
1   green pepper, chopped
    chopped green chilies (optional)
2   ripe tomatoes, chopped
½   head of lettuce, chopped
    sprouts
1   recipe tomato salsa* (page 183)
    plain low-fat yogurt* (page 114)
        (optional)

Spread tortillas on a teflon baking sheet. Place
ground round lengthwise in the center of each
tortilla. Cover meat with cheese. Top cheese with
onions, green pepper, green chilies and tomatoes.
Bake at 400° for 10-15 minutes or until cheese
melts. Remove from oven. Top with lettuce, sprouts
and salsa. Fold left and right edges of tortilla over
center to cover filling. Top with yogurt.

CHILI CON CARNE

1   pound extra-lean ground round
1   onion, chopped
2   cloves garlic, minced
1   28-oz. can tomatoes
½   teaspoon ground cumin
1   teaspoon cayenne pepper
1   tablespoon chili powder
4   cups cooked kidney beans or two
     15-oz. cans red kidney beans
     with liquid
2   cups macaroni, cooked
1   7-oz. can chopped green chilies
     (optional)

Brown ground beef with onions and garlic; drain off any excess fat. Add tomatoes and seasonings; simmer uncovered 1½-2 hours. Add kidney beans; heat to boiling. Add macaroni; heat to serving temperature. Sprinkle with green chilies.

Note: This recipe is very hot. For a milder flavor, reduce the cumin and the cayenne.

BEEF STROGANOFF

1 pound extra-lean ground round
¾ cup onion, finely chopped
1 clove garlic, minced
½ pound fresh mushrooms, sliced
¼ teaspoon or less salt
⅛ teaspoon pepper
⅛ teaspoon rosemary
2 tablespoons flour
1½ cups cream of chicken soup*
    (page 158)
1 cup plain low-fat yogurt* (page 114)
1 1-pound package bowtie-shaped
    pasta, cooked
  poppy seeds
  fresh parsley for garnish

Sauté ground beef, onion and garlic; drain off any excess fat. Add mushrooms; cook 3-5 minutes. Stir in salt, pepper, rosemary and flour; simmer uncovered 10 minutes. Add soup and heat. Stir in yogurt; heat, but do not boil. Arrange pasta around edges of large platter; spoon stroganoff into center. Sprinkle pasta with poppy seeds. Garnish with fresh parsley.

271

PIZZA

Crust

2   teaspoons dried yeast
¾   cup warm water
4   cups flour
½   teaspoon sugar
½   teaspoon salt
2   tablespoons olive oil
1   egg or ¼ cup egg substitute, beaten

Dissolve yeast in ¾ cup warm water. Mix flour with sugar and salt; add to yeast along with oil and egg and stir until mixed. Knead on a heavily floured board until smooth and elastic. (Add additional water if needed for moisture.) Put dough in a bowl greased with tub safflower margarine; cover and let rise in a warm place for 1 hour. Punch down. Knead slightly. Let rise 1 more hour. Divide dough in half. Roll into two 9-inch crusts. Dough may be frozen.

Sauce per Crust

1   1-lb. can plum tomatoes
1   tablespoon tomato paste
1   tablespoon olive oil
¼   teaspoon oregano
¼   teaspoon basil
¼   teaspoon pepper
½   lb. grated Mozzarella cheese

Drain tomatoes; dice. Reserve ½ cup of the juice; mix juice with tomato paste, diced tomatoes and olive oil. Spread over crust; sprinkle with oregano, basil and pepper. Add choice of toppings.
Continued

Toppings:
      fresh ripe tomatoes
      sautéed onions
      fresh mushrooms, sliced and
         steamed 2-3 minutes
      green onions
      green chili peppers
      extra-lean ground round,
         cooked and drained
      cooked chicken
      chopped clams
      fresh pineapple
      sprouts

Sprinkle with cheese. Bake at 450° for 20 minutes or until crust is done and cheese is melted.

LASAGNA

1½-2	pounds extra-lean ground round
1	clove garlic
1	small onion
3	pounds canned plum tomatoes
3½	teaspoons safflower oil
3½	teaspoons olive oil
1	24-oz. can tomato sauce
½	teaspoon or less salt
½	teaspoon oregano
1	teaspoon basil
¼	teaspoon pepper
2	bunches fresh spinach
2	cups Ricotta cheese
1	package lasagna, cooked and drained crushed red pepper
½-¾	lbs. thinly sliced Mozzarella cheese

Brown ground round with garlic and onion in a teflon skillet; drain excess fat. Set aside. Purée tomatoes in blender; add oils, tomato sauce and spices. Whirl 2-3 minutes. Set aside. Wash spinach; shake dry and remove any tough lower stems. Steam in a covered skillet 2-3 minutes or until wilted. Squeeze dry; chop. Combine spinach, ground round and Ricotta

Cover bottom of a 13"x9"x2" pan with tomato sauce. Add a layer of pasta. Spread with spinach mixture. Sprinkle with red pepper. Add a layer of Mozzarella. Cover with sauce. Repeat layers 2-3 more times. Pour remaining sauce over final layer. Top with additional cheese. Bake covered at 350° for 45-60 minutes. Serves 8-10.

Note: For a smaller group use two 8-inch square pans and put one in the freezer.

CHAPTER NINETEEN

DESSERTS

Note: Because sugar reduction is essential to good cardiac health, desserts should be used sparingly, and only for very special occasions.

Remember, the premier dessert is fresh fruit.

APPLESAUCE

8-10 large cooking apples, peeled, cored and cut into chunks
½ cup water
½ cup or less sugar
1 teaspoon cinnamon

Put apples and water in saucepan; cover and simmer, stirring frequently, until apples are barely tender. Add sugar and continue cooking about 30 minutes or until sugar dissolves. Stir in cinnamon.

Note: For a smooth, rather than a chunky type sauce, purée apples in the blender or food processor before adding sugar. Proceed as for chunky style.

If using a crock pot, combine all ingredients. Cover. Cook on low 8 hours or overnight.

BAKED APPLES

¼ cup or less brown sugar
1 teaspoon cinnamon
1 tablespoon safflower oil
⅓ cup raisins
6-8 medium baking apples

Mix sugar, cinnamon, oil and raisins. Fill center of apples. Place upright in baking dish. Pour 1 cup water around apples. Bake at 375° 45-60 minutes, basting frequently.

Note: If using a crock pot, reduce water to ½ cup. Cook on low 8 hours or overnight.

BAKED APRICOTS

    fresh apricots, halved and pitted
2   teaspoons water per apricot
    vanilla sugar (instructions follow)
    plain low-fat yogurt* (page 114)

Place apricots and water in a baking dish; sprinkle with vanilla sugar. Bake in a 375° oven for 30-35 minutes. Garnish with a dollop of low-fat yogurt.

Vanilla Sugar: Store 2 vanilla beans with 2 cups sugar in a covered jar for several weeks. The longer it is stored, the better the flavor.

BROILED PAPAYA HALVES

1-2   fresh papayas
      fresh lime juice
      wedges of fresh lime

Cut papayas in half lengthwise. Remove seeds. Brush with lime juice. Place skin side down on broiler rack; cook 2-3 minutes. Serve with lime wedges.

Note: To barbecue, place split papayas on edge of barbecue, grill 5-6 minutes — just until hot.

BAKED BANANAS

1½   teaspoons fresh lemon juice
1   teaspoon grated lemon rind
1   tablespoon brown sugar
4   bananas, peeled and sliced
      lengthwise

Combine lemon juice, lemon rind and brown sugar; brush over bananas. Bake at 375° for 15 minutes. Serve at once.

BANANAS WITH HONEY AND BROWN SUGAR

Peel bananas and place in baking dish. Drizzle with honey; sprinkle with brown sugar. Top with nuts, if desired. Bake at 375° for 15 minutes.

POACHED PEARS

1   cup white wine
1   vanilla bean, split open
4-6 firm, ripe pears
¼   cup lemon juice
2   tablespoons orange juice
     fresh mint for garnish
     fresh fruits for garnish

Place wine and vanilla bean in medium saucepan; bring to a boil. Peel and quarter pears; dip in lemon juice. Place pears in vegetable steamer over boiling wine; cover and steam 8-10 minutes or until tender. Remove from pan. Boil poaching liquid 2-3 minutes to reduce. Remove and discard vanilla bean. Combine 2 tablespoons poaching liquid with 2 tablespoons lemon juice and 2 tablespoons orange juice.

Serve pears at room temperature on individual dessert plates with a small amount of sauce. Garnish with fresh mint and fresh fruits in season, such as sliced fresh peaches (dip in lemon juice to preserve color), grapes, kiwi, bananas, cantaloupe, watermelon, plums, peeled orange segments or mandarin oranges.

FROZEN WATERMELON

Layer slices of watermelon in a 13"x9"x2" pan; cover with plastic wrap and freeze 30 minutes. Turn. Return to freezer until ready to serve. Garnish with sherbets, sorbets or ices, or fresh fruits and sprigs of mint.

RHUBARB SAUCE

4 cups rhubarb, cut into 1-inch slices
½ cup sugar or 4 tablespoons honey
1-2 tablespoons water

Combine all ingredients in a saucepan; cover. Cook slowly about 10 minutes or until fruit is tender.

Variations: Warm, serve over sliced bananas. Or serve with Yogurt Topping — combine 1 cup plain low-fat yogurt* (page 114) with the juice and rind of ½ lemon; add a dash of honey.

APPLE CRISP

6-7 tart cooking apples
1 tablespoon lemon juice
⅓ cup granulated sugar
1 teaspoon cinnamon
¾ cup rolled oats
½ cup flour
1 cup brown sugar
3 tablespoons safflower oil

Place apples in a deep baking dish; sprinkle with lemon juice, sugar and cinnamon. Combine remaining ingredients; pour over apples. Bake at 375° for 30 minutes or until apples are tender.

SINGLE PASTRY CRUST

1½ cups all-purpose flour
1½ teaspoons sugar
¾ teaspoon salt
½ cup safflower oil
2 tablespoons skim milk

Combine flour, sugar and salt. Mix together oil and milk; add to flour. Using a pastry blender or fork, work mixture into a soft dough. Add additional milk if needed. Form into a ball. Roll out on a well-floured pastry cloth. Place in a 9" pie plate. Adjust crust. Flute edges.

Note: If a baked shell is needed, prick bottom and sides of crust with a fork. Bake at 450° 10-12 minutes or until golden. If filling and crust are to be baked together, do not prick crust.

DOUBLE PASTRY CRUST

2 cups all-purpose flour
½ teaspoon salt
4 tablespoons ice water
⅔ cup safflower mayonnaise
1½ tablespoons skim milk

Combine flour and salt. Mix ice water with mayonnaise; add to flour. Using a pastry blender or fork, work mixture together; add milk. Form into a ball. Divide dough in half. Roll out on a well-floured pastry cloth. Place in a 9" pie plate; adjust crust. Fill. Add top crust; flute edges.

Note: It is very important that the ice water be ice cold.

STRAWBERRY-RHUBARB PIE

- ½ cup sugar
- ¼ cup flour
- ¼ teaspoon salt
- ¼ teaspoon nutmeg
- 3 cups rhubarb, cut into ½-inch pieces
- 1 cup strawberries, sliced
- 1 9-inch double pastry crust* (page 282)

Combine sugar, flour, salt and nutmeg. Add fruit. Toss to coat. Let stand 20 minutes. Spoon into pastry-lined pie plate. Adjust top crust. Flute edges. Prick. Bake at 400° 40-45 minutes.

FRESH BERRY PIE

- 1 9-inch double pastry crust* (page 282)
- 2 tablespoons flour
- ½ cup sugar
- ⅛ teaspoon salt
- 4 cups fresh raspberries, strawberries, or blackberries
- 1 teaspoon lemon juice

Line a 9-inch pie plate with pastry. Mix together flour, sugar and salt; sprinkle ¼ of the mixture on uncooked bottom crust. Coat berries with lemon juice and toss with remaining sugar mixture. Spoon into pie plate. Adjust top crust; flute edges. Prick. Bake at 450° for 15 minutes. Reduce heat to 350° and continue baking 25-30 minutes.

APPLE PIE

6 cups apples, pared and sliced
1¼ tablespoons lemon juice
¼ cup sugar
½ teaspoon cinnamon
⅛ teaspoon salt
2 tablespoons flour
1 9-inch double pastry crust* (page 282)

Toss apples with lemon juice. Combine sugar, salt, cinnamon and flour; mix with apples. Spoon into pastry-lined pie plate. Adjust top crust. Flute edges. Prick. Bake at 450° for 10 minutes. Reduce heat to 375° and continue baking 40-50 minutes.

TOPPING FOR FRUIT COBBLER

1 cup all-purpose flour, sifted
½ teaspoon salt
1½ teaspoons baking powder
⅓ cup skim milk
3 tablespoons safflower oil

Combine flour, salt and baking powder. Mix milk with oil; add to flour. Using a fork or pastry blender, work dough into a ball. Drop by spoonfuls onto fruit cobbler. (Recipes follow.)

BERRY COBBLER

- ¾ cup water
- 2 tablespoons cornstarch
- ½ cup sugar
- 3 cups strawberries, raspberries,
  blueberries or blackberries
- 1 recipe cobbler topping*

In medium saucepan, combine water, cornflour and sugar; bring to a boil. Cook for 1 minute, stirring constantly. Add berries and remove from heat. Pour into a 9-inch or a 10-inch pie plate. Top with cobbler topping. Bake at 425° 25-30 minutes or until topping is lightly browned.

CHERRY COBBLER

1   20-oz. can pitted, tart pie cherries
      with liquid
½   cup sugar
1   tablespoon minute tapioca
1   recipe cobbler topping* (page 284)

Combine cherries, sugar and tapioca in medium
saucepan; cook, stirring constantly until sugar is
dissolved and syrup is clear. Pour into a 9-inch or
a 10-inch pie plate. Dot with cobbler topping. Bake
at 425° 25-30 minutes or until topping is lightly
browned.

RHUBARB COBBLER

4   cups rhubarb, cut into 1–inch pieces
½   cup sugar
1-2   tablespoons water
2   tablespoons cornstarch
1   recipe cobbler topping* (page 284)

In medium saucepan, combine rhubarb, sugar,
water and cornstarch. Bring to a boil; cook for 1
minute, stirring constantly. Pour into a 9-inch or a
10-inch pie plate. Dot with cobbler topping. Bake
at 425° 25-30 minutes or until topping is lightly
browned.

FREEZING AND BEATING ICES

Pour mixture into large mixing bowl suitable for freezing. Cover. Freeze 1-2 hours or until solid around edges, but still slightly slushy in center. Remove from freezer. Beat with electric mixer on medium speed until mixture is smooth and no large crystals remain. Cover. Refreeze for 1 hour. Serve at once or refreeze. If refrozen, allow mixture to soften 5-10 minutes at room temperature or for 30 minutes at refrigerator temperature before serving.

Note: It is important that the bowl used for freezing be large because the mixture must not be too deep if it is to freeze properly. When doubling a recipe, use 2 bowls, rather than one.

Serve ices in chilled, stemmed glasses, in fresh lemon or orange shells, in cantaloupe or other melon boats. Garnish with whole fresh fruits and a sprig of mint.

FRESH STRAWBERRY ICE

4   cups hulled strawberries
1½   teaspoons lemon juice
2   teaspoons sugar

Purée berries in blender; add lemon juice and sugar and whirl 2-3 minutes. Pour into large bowl. Follow preceding instructions for freezing and beating ices.

LEMON ICE

2 cups water
2½ tablespoons sugar
½ cup fresh lemon juice
grated rinds of 2 lemons

Combine water and sugar in saucepan; boil without stirring for 5 minutes. Cool. Add lemon juice and rind; stir. Pour into large bowl suitable for freezing. Follow instructions for freezing and beating ices (page 287).

To Serve: Cut tops from whole lemons; squeeze out juice (reserve for lemon ice or for lemonade). Remove pulp. Fill shells with lemon ice. Garnish with violets or with blueberries and a sprig of mint.

LIME ICE

2 cups water
½ cup sugar
1 cup fresh lime juice
juice of 1 orange

Combine water and sugar in medium saucepan; boil without stirring for 5 minutes. Cool. Add lime juice and orange juice. Pour into a large mixing bowl suitable for freezing. Follow instructions for freezing and beating ices (page 287).

To Serve: Cut tops from whole limes; squeeze out juice (reserve for limeade). Remove pulp. Fill shells with lime ice. Garnish with sliced papaya or peeled orange segments and a sprig of fresh mint.

WATERMELON ICE

3   cups watermelon pulp
⅓   cup sugar
    juice of 1 large orange

Purée watermelon pulp in blender; add remaining ingredients and whirl 3-4 minutes. Pour into large mixing bowl suitable for freezing. Follow instructions for freezing and beating ices* (page 287).

To Serve: Spoon over cantaloupe or honeydew boats. Garnish with fresh mint.

PAPAYA ICE

2   ripe papayas, peeled
2   tablespoons sugar
⅓   cup water
2   tablespoons fresh lime juice

Purée papaya in blender. Combine sugar and water in saucepan; boil 5 minutes without stirring. Cool to room temperature. Pour lime juice over papaya. Add cooled syrup. Whirl in blender 3-4 minutes. Pour into large mixing bowl suitable for freezing. Follow instructions for freezing and beating ices* (page 287).

PINEAPPLE ICE

3 cups unsweetened pineapple juice

Pour juice into blender; whirl 3-4 minutes. Pour into large mixing bowl suitable for freezing. Follow instructions for freezing and beating ices* (page 287).

KIWI ICE

2 cups peeled kiwi
½ teaspoon lemon juice
¼ cup water
¼ cup sugar

Purée kiwi in blender; add remaining ingredients and whirl 2-3 minutes. Pour into large mixing bowl suitable for freezing. Follow instructions for freezing and beating ices* (page 287).

GRANITA DE CAFÈ CON PANE

2 cups decaffeinated espresso coffee
3 teaspoons sugar or lightly to taste
1 recipe whipped cream substitute*
(page 114)

Combine brewed coffee and sugar. Pour into large mixing bowl suitable for freezing. Follow instructions for freezing and beating ices* (page 287).

To Serve: Spoon into stemmed glasses. Garnish with whipped cream substitute.

FREEZING AND BEATING SORBETS

Pour mixture into large mixing bowl suitable for freezing. Cover. Freeze 1-2 hours or until solid around edges but still slightly slushy in center; remove from freezer. Beat until smooth and no large crystals remain. Set aside. In small mixing bowl, beat egg whites. Fold into sorbets. Return to freezer. Freeze without stirring 1-2 hours.

*Note: It is important that the bowl used for freezing be large because the mixture must not be too deep if it is to freeze properly. When doubling a recipe, use 2 bowls, rather than one.

The amount of sugar may be varied depending on the sweetness of the fruit. If additional sugar is necessary, add it to the egg whites before beating.

For creamier sorbet, add an additional egg white.

These sorbets have a good texture and will keep a long while in the freezer.

WATERMELON SORBET

- 3 cups watermelon pulp, puréed in blender
- ⅓ cup sugar or lightly to taste
  juice of 1 large orange
- 2 egg whites, beaten until stiff

Combine watermelon purée, sugar and orange juice. Pour into large bowl. Follow preceding instructions for freezing and beating sorbets.

LEMON SORBET

1   cup fresh lemon juice
    grated rind of 3 lemons
2   cups water
½   cup sugar
3   egg whites, beaten until frothy

Combine water and sugar in medium saucepan; boil without stirring for 5 minutes. Cool. Add lemon juice. Pour into blender; whirl 3 minutes. Pour into large mixing bowl. Follow instructions for freezing and beating sorbets* (page 291).

Note: To make Lime Sorbet, substitute lime juice for lemon juice and add the juice of 1 orange. Omit the grated rind of 3 lemons.

PAPAYA SORBET

2   ripe papayas, peeled
3   tablespoons sugar
⅓   cup water
2   tablespoons fresh lime juice
2   egg whites, beaten until frothy

Purée papaya in blender. Combine sugar and water in medium saucepan; boil 5 minutes without stirring. Cool to room temperature. Pour lime juice over papaya. Add cooled syrup. Pour into blender; whirl 3 minutes. Pour into large mixing bowl. Follow instructions for freezing and beating sorbets* (page 291).

VANILLA ICE CREAM

2 cups skim milk
  scant tablespoon powdered gelatin
1¼ cups sugar
2 cups evaporated milk
1½ teaspoons vanilla essence

Heat skim milk just to scalding; do not boil. Remove from heat; stir in gelatin and sugar. Stir until dissolved. Pour into blender. Whirl 3-5 minutes. Add evaporated milk; whirl 2 minutes. Chill 5 hours or overnight. Process in ice cream freezer according to manufacturer's directions. Stir in vanilla essence. Chill 30-60 minutes.

Variations: Just before serving, top with fresh berries or with blueberry* or raspberry sauce* (page 145).

CHOCOLATE ICE CREAM: Add 6 tablespoons unsweetened cocoa powder and ¼-½ teaspoon cinnamon to vanilla recipe.

ROCKY ROAD ICE CREAM: Prepare chocolate ice cream. After processing add ¾ cup miniature marshmallows.

COFFEE ICE CREAM: Prepare vanilla ice cream. Add 2 tablespoons decaffeinated instant coffee powder when stirring in the gelatin and sugar. Process as directed. Then add 1½ tablespoons finely ground, decaffeinated espresso coffee.

PECAN ICE CREAM: Prepare vanilla ice cream. After processing add 1 cup whole pecans.
Continued

FRESH PEACH ICE CREAM: Prepare vanilla ice cream, substituting ¼ teaspoon almond extract for vanilla. Purée 3 ripe, peeled peaches in blender. Peel and slice 2 additional peaches. Stir into processed recipe. Chill.

FRESH STRAWBERRY, RASPBERRY, BLUEBERRY OR BLACKBERRY ICE CREAM: Prepare vanilla ice cream. Process. Purée 2 cups fresh berries in blender. Slice an additional 1 cup of berries. Fold into processed recipe. Chill.

FRESH CHERRY ICE CREAM: Prepare strawberry ice cream. Substitute pitted cherries for berries.

FRESH APRICOT OR PLUM ICE CREAM: Prepare strawberry ice cream. Substitute plums or apricots for berries.

PEANUT BUTTER COOKIES

    4   egg whites
    2   cups non-hydrogenated peanut
          butter
  1⅔   cups granulated sugar

Beat egg whites until stiff. Set aside. Combine peanut butter and sugar; fold in egg whites. Drop by teaspoonfuls onto teflon baking sheets. Flatten slightly with prongs of fork. Bake at 325° for 20 minutes. Remove to wire racks to cool.

MOLASSES COOKIES

2	cups all-purpose flour
¼	teaspoon salt
1	teaspoon baking powder
1	teaspoon baking soda
½	teaspoon ground cloves
1¼	teaspoon ground ginger
1¼	teaspoon cinnamon
⅔	cup safflower oil
¼	cup molasses
1	egg or ¼ cup egg substitute
1	cup firmly packed brown sugar
	granulated sugar

Sift together flour, salt, baking powder, baking soda, cloves, ginger and cinnamon. Set aside. Using lowest speed of electric mixer, blend oil, molasses and egg; add sugar. Blend. Gradually add flour and dry ingredients; mix well.

Chill dough 2 hours. Form into 1-inch balls. Roll each ball in granulated sugar. Place on teflon baking sheets. Sprinkle each cookie with 2-3 drops of water. Bake at 375° 8-10 minutes.

RAISIN-OATMEAL COOKIES

1	orange with rind
6	tablespoons safflower oil
¾	cup honey
½	cup skim milk
2	teaspoons vanilla essence
1	cup whole wheat pastry flour
1½	cups rolled oats
½	teaspoon baking soda
½	teaspoon salt
½	teaspoon baking powder
1	teaspoon cinnamon
1	teaspoon nutmeg
1½	cups raisins

Grind orange with rind in grinder or blender; add oil, honey, milk and vanilla essence; blend. Combine remaining ingredients; add to orange mixture. Stir to blend. Drop by large serving-spoonfuls onto teflon baking sheets. Bake at 300° for 25-30 minutes. Remove to wire racks to cool.

Note: If less orange flavor is desired, use less orange rind.

For smaller cookies, drop by teaspoonfuls.

YELLOW CHIFFON CAKE

2 eggs, separated
1¼ cups sugar
2¼ cups flour
3 teaspoons baking powder
¾ teaspoon salt
⅓ cup safflower oil
1 cup skim milk
1½ teaspoons vanilla essence

Beat egg whites until frothy. Gradually add ½ cup sugar; beat until egg whites are stiff. Set aside. In large bowl, sift together remaining sugar, flour, baking powder and salt; add oil, ½ of the milk and vanilla essence. Beat 1 minute on medium speed; add remaining milk and egg yolks. Beat 1 minute longer. Gently fold in egg whites. Bake in teflon cake pans at 350° for 30-35 minutes.

SEVEN MINUTE ICING

2 egg whites
1¼ cups sugar
½ cup water
¼ teaspoon cream of tartar
1 teaspoon vanilla essence

Bring 2 cups water to a boil in bottom of double boiler. In top of double boiler, combine egg whites, sugar, water and cream of tartar; beat 1 minute. Place over boiling water. Using highest speed of electric mixer, beat constantly 5-7 minutes or until frosting stands in stiff peaks. Remove from heat. Stir in vanilla essence.

CHOCOLATE CAKE

2	eggs, separated
1¼	cups sugar
1¾	cups flour
¾	teaspoon baking soda
¾	teaspoon salt
½	cup safflower oil
1	cup skim milk plus 1 tablespoon vinegar
¼	cup unsweetened cocoa powder
½	teaspoon vanilla essence

Beat egg whites until frothy. Gradually beat in ½ cup sugar; beat until egg whites are stiff. Set aside. In large mixing bowl, sift together remaining sugar, flour, baking soda and salt; add oil, ½ of the milk and vanilla essence. Beat one minute on medium speed; add remaining milk, egg yolks and cocoa powder. Beat 1 minute longer. Fold in egg whites. Bake in teflon cake pans or in paper-lined muffin cups at 350° for 30–35 minutes. Cool on wire racks.

CHOCOLATE-FUDGE CAKE

2 cups flour
1¼ cups sugar
½ cup unsweetened cocoa powder
½ teaspoon salt
1 tablespoon baking soda
⅔ cup safflower oil
1 cup skim milk
1 cup strong decaffeinated coffee

Combine flour, sugar, cocoa, salt and baking soda; add oil and milk and blend with a spoon. Stir in boiling coffee. Pour into an 8-inch square teflon baking pan, into paper-lined muffin cups or into a 9-inch round teflon baking pan. Bake at 350° for 35-40 minutes. Cool on wire racks. Frost with chocolate fudge frosting* (recipe below).

CHOCOLATE-FUDGE FROSTING

3 tablespoons unsweetened cocoa powder
1 cup sugar
⅓ cup evaporated milk
3 tablespoons safflower oil
1 teaspoon vanilla essence

In medium saucepan, combine all ingredients, except vanilla essence. Bring to a boil, reduce heat and simmer 1 minute. Remove from heat. Add vanilla essence, beat 5 minutes. Spread over cake.

Note: Add additional milk or water if needed for a creamier spreading consistency.

SOURCE NOTES

The chart on the fat content of fast foods is based upon information from "On the Fast Food Trail," by Wendy Midgley, R.D. (*Diabetes Forecast* July/August 1979), and is used with permission of the American Diabetes Association, copyright 1979; and from "How Good Are Fast Foods," by Jane E. Brody (*New York Times*, Sept. 19, 1979) and is used with permission of The New York Times Company, copyright 1979.

INDEX

302

303